All About® Reading

The program that takes the struggle out of reading

Pre-reading

by Marie Rippel

Copyright © 2012, 2011 by All About® Learning Press, Inc.
Printed in the United States of America

All About® Learning Press, Inc.
615 Commerce Loop
Eagle River, WI 54521

ISBN 978-1-935197-18-8
v. 1.0

Editor: Renée LaTulippe
Cover Design: David LaTulippe
Page Layout: Renée LaTulippe
Illustrations: Mike Eustis and Donna Goeddaeus

The *All About Reading* Pre-reading Teacher's Manual
is part of the *All About*® *Reading* program.

For more books in this series, go to www.AllAboutReading.com.

Dear Parents and Teachers,

This program is unique. From your children's point of view, they are playing games, doing craft sheets, and listening to good stories. But although your children may feel that they are playing, something else is going on. As they engage in the activities, they will be absorbing critical pre-reading skills almost effortlessly.

Thirty-four percent of children have difficulty learning to read. This number is especially tragic because research and experience show that there is much that you can do during the preschool and kindergarten years to prepare your child for reading. The preparation you do at this early stage prevents struggles later on.

There are five important pre-reading skills. These components are so important to your child's future reading and spelling ability that we call them the Big Five Skills™. Teaching the Big Five Skills™ is the most important step you can take to show your child how to love and understand the printed word.

And this is the part that I like best: these activities are so much fun for you and your children to do together that it'll never seem like "work." May you enjoy this time with your children, and take pleasure in watching them expand their world.

Contents

3 The Sounds of the Letters

4 Appendices

What Do You Need?

In addition to this Teacher's Manual, you will need the following items:

Student Material Packet

The Student Material Packet contains:
- *My Book of Letters* activity book
- Capital Letter Alphabet Chart
- Lowercase Letter Alphabet Chart
- Picture Cards and Letter Sound Cards

Interactive Kit

The Interactive Kit contains:
- Activity Box and divider cards
- *Letter Sounds A to Z* CD-ROM
- Ziggy Zebra puppet
- Tote Bag

Readers
- *The Zigzag Zebra* book
  (Optional audio book is also available)
- *Lizard Lou* book
  (Optional audio book is also available)

Common Craft Materials
- Crayons
- Markers
- Scissors
- Glue
- Tape
- Other optional craft materials as indicated on the ABC Craft Sheets in *My Book of Letters*

Get Set Up in Four Easy Steps

1. **Alphabet Charts:** There are two alphabet charts in your Student Material Packet. The Capital Letter Chart will be used in Lessons 1–26, and the Lowercase Letter Chart will be used in Lessons 27–52. Consider displaying the alphabet chart you are using on the wall, refrigerator, or the back of a door.

2. ***My Book of Letters* activity book:** The pages in this activity book are perforated and can be removed from the book as you need them. Each lesson will tell you which page you need. (Look for the "You Will Need" section at the beginning of the lesson.)

3. **Picture Cards** and **Letter Sound Cards:** These activity cards are perforated. Separate the cards and insert them behind the appropriate dividers in your **Activity Box**.

4. **Tote bag:** With the exception of the Lowercase Letter Chart, store all items in your tote bag. The lesson plans will tell you when you need specific items.

The Importance of the Big Five Skills™

The Big Five Skills™ are the five most important pre-reading skills for young children:

1. Print Awareness
2. Phonological Awareness
3. Letter Knowledge
4. Listening Comprehension
5. Motivation to Read

These five components form the foundation for your child's future reading and spelling ability. *All About Reading* Pre-1 teaches all five of these essential skills so your children will have the best possible start when they begin reading.

Print Awareness is the most basic of the Big Five Skills™. It is the understanding that text carries meaning and is related to spoken language. The greater the child's awareness of print, the more quickly and easily he or she can learn to read. Specific tips for developing print awareness are included in the lessons.

Phonological Awareness is the ability to hear and identify parts of words. As the child interacts with the puppet, Ziggy, and tries out different language-based games, he is learning to pay attention to various parts of words (the ending sound, the beginning sound, or the rhyme). He's learning how to take words apart and put them back together again.

The ability to attend to the various sounds in words is extremely important when it comes to learning to read. Research shows us that children who have strong phonological awareness learn to read much more easily, and their first attempts at learning to read can be successful. This early advantage sticks with the child as he continues through his school career.

Letter Knowledge is recognizing the letters and knowing the letter names and sounds. Your child will gain a new awareness of letters as he works on the alphabet craft sheets, experiments with letter sounds, and eventually matches those sounds with specific letters.

Listening Comprehension is a precursor to reading comprehension. We foster listening comprehension by discussing stories and characters, expanding vocabulary, and exposing children to a wide variety of experiences. Additionally, through *The Zigzag Zebra*, *Lizard Lou*, and the read-alouds, the child absorbs language patterns that are not used as frequently in normal conversation but are commonly used in books.

Motivation to Read is gained through interesting and varied reading experiences. Also called print motivation, the concept is that the child *wants* to learn to read. The child who has motivation to read has gotten the message that "Reading is fun, and it's something I want to do soon!"

Simple ABC activities are not enough to ensure your children's eventual success. Your children need every one of these Big Five Skills™ to thrive once reading instruction begins, so these foundational skills are taught in every lesson of this book. You'll find that these lessons are presented in a child-friendly way, with simple, easy, play-like activities.

Part 1
Capital Letters

Tips for Part 1 (Lessons 1–26)

- **Complete the lessons at your child's own pace.** You might choose to complete one lesson per day or one lesson per week.

- **Keep *The Zigzag Zebra* book handy.** You'll be reading a short selection from this book each day. *The Zigzag Zebra* was specially written to include rhyme, alliteration, and rhythm, which all support phonological awareness. At the same time, each verse features the Letter of the Day, helping your child develop letter awareness.

- **The ABC Craft Sheets are perforated and can be removed from *My Book of Letters*.** The craft sheets are related to the day's reading from *The Zigzag Zebra*. As children interact with the letters, they soak up information about the featured letter of the alphabet: the shape of the letter, the name of the letter, and, subconsciously, the sound of the letter.

- **Get ready for fun with Ziggy the Zebra puppet!** Ziggy helps you present many of the Language Exploration games.

- **Plan time for the Read-Aloud Time.** See page 17 for ideas for fitting this important activity into your day.

Lesson 1 - Capital A

This lesson will teach capital letter A and a rhyming game.

You will need: *My Book of Letters* page 5

Letter of the Day

Read the article "The Alphabet Song" on page 197 for important tips.

Knowing the Alphabet Song is one of the first indicators of print awareness, one of the Big Five Skills™.

Sing the Alphabet Song

Sing the Alphabet Song with your child. Point to the letters on the Capital Letter Chart as each letter is named.

"Today's letter is A!" Have your child find the letter A on the letter chart.

Complete Letter Activities for Capital A

Read the poem for the letter A on pages 7-10 of *The Zigzag Zebra*.

See if your child can locate the capital A in the text on page 10.

Have your child do the ABC Craft Sheet for capital letter A.

Choose one or more activities from page 195 and complete them with your child.

Play "Rhyming Body Parts" with Ziggy

Take out the Ziggy Zebra puppet and put it on. Introduce Ziggy Zebra to your child and explain that he is a young zebra who sometimes says the wrong word. If Ziggy says the wrong word, the child should tell him the right word.

Puppet: "Let's play a game together. I will point to a body part and tell you what it is. If I say it wrong, you tell me the right word."

Use Ziggy Zebra to point to the parts on your child, following the dialogue below.

This game is an introduction to the concept of rhyming.

If your child doesn't grasp the idea of rhyming right away, that is fine. There are more rhyming activities in future lessons.

Rhyming encourages phonological awareness, a Big Five Skill™.

Point to:	Ziggy says:	Your child says:
shoulder	"This is your *holder*."	*No, it's my* **shoulder**!
hand	"Then this is your *land*."	*No, it's my* **hand**!
finger	"Is this your *linger*?"	*No, it's my* **finger**!
mouth	"But this is your *south*."	*No, it's my* **mouth**!
arm	"Well, this is your *farm*."	*No, it's my* **arm**!
knee	"Is this your *key*?"	*No, it's my* **knee**!
leg	"I know this is your *egg*."	*No, it's my* **leg**!
eye	"This must be your *sky*."	*No, it's my* **eye**!
big toe	"This is your big *snow*."	*No, it's my big* **toe**!
ear	"For sure this is your *deer*."	*No, it's my* **ear**!
foot	"Then this is your *put*."	*No, it's my* **foot**!
back	"So is this your *sack*?"	*No, it's my* **back**!
chin	"And this is your *chin*."	*Yes! It's my* **chin**!

"Hooray! I got one right!"

Lesson 1: Capital A

Read-Aloud Time   Read a Story or Poem

Read aloud to your child for twenty minutes.

 The best thing you can do when it comes to reading aloud is to make read-aloud time a normal part of your child's daily routine. When you make reading aloud a priority, you will log more read-aloud hours each week, and your child will benefit greatly.

Twenty minutes a day will amount to 10 hours a month and 120 hours a year. If you start reading books aloud when your child is one year old, by the time the child turns six he has listened to 600 hours of delightful stories, factual accounts, and fantastic storylines. The child's head is filled with information about people and places near and far, proper grammar, and the rhythm and patterns of language. What a great starting place for learning to read independently!

One easy way to remember read-aloud time is to tie it to something else that you already do every day. You probably already tuck your child in bed, so that is a natural time to read. You already eat breakfast (or at least drink a cup of coffee), so perhaps you can fit in the 20 minutes right after eating. If you're the type who's consistent about following a written schedule, plug read-aloud time right into its own block of time.

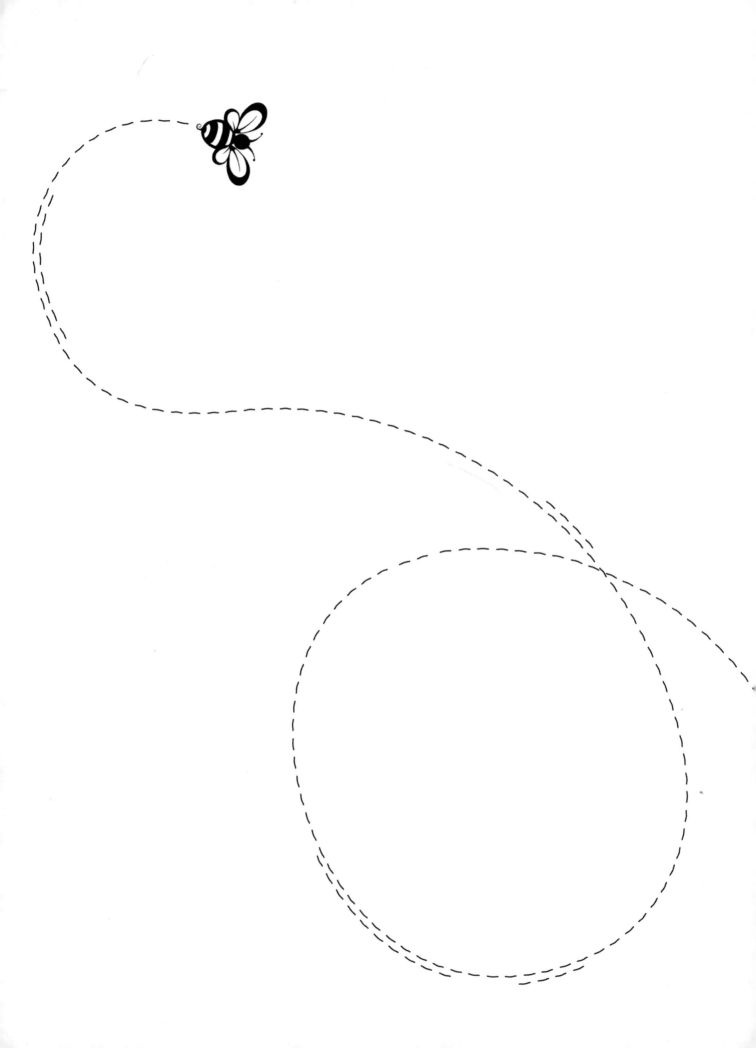

Lesson 2 - Capital B

This lesson will teach capital letter B and a new rhyming game.

You will need: *My Book of Letters* page 7, Picture Cards for Lesson 2

Letter of the Day   Sing the Alphabet Song

Sing the Alphabet Song with your child. Point to the letters on the Capital Letter Chart as each letter is named.

"Today's letter is B!" Have your child find the letter B on the letter chart.

Complete Letter Activities for Capital B

Read the poem for the letter B on pages 11-14 of *The Zigzag Zebra.*

See if your child can locate the capital B in the text on pages 13 and 14.

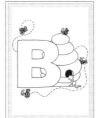

Have your child do the ABC Craft Sheet for capital letter B.

Choose one or more activities from page 195 and complete them with your child.

Language Exploration

Play "Rhyming Cards"

Take out the Picture Cards for Lesson 2 from your Activity Box. Make sure your child understands what each picture represents.

duck	truck	boat	goat	clock	sock

| rake | cake | king | ring | fox | box |

Lay *duck* and *truck* next to each other.

Explain that when words sound the same at the end, like *duck* and *truck*, they rhyme.

Mix up the remaining Picture Cards and have your child find the pairs that rhyme.

> If your child needs extra help with this activity, use the following dialogue: **Tip!**
>
> "Say this word with me: *boat*." *Boat.*
>
> "Help me find the picture that rhymes with *boat*. -Oat, -oat, -oat. What sounds like -oat at the end?" *Child finds the* goat.
>
> "Good! *Boat* and *goat* sound the same at the end, so they rhyme."

Read-Aloud Time ## Read a Story or Poem

Read aloud to your child for twenty minutes.

Lesson 3 - Capital C

This lesson will teach capital letter C and a new rhyming game.

You will need: *My Book of Letters* pages 9 and 11, Picture Cards for Lesson 3

Letter of the Day   Sing the Alphabet Song

Sing the Alphabet Song with your child. Point to the letters on the Capital Letter Chart as each letter is named.

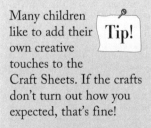

"Today's letter is C!" Have your child find the letter C on the letter chart.

Complete Letter Activities for Capital C

Read the poem for the letter C on pages 15-18 of *The Zigzag Zebra*.

See if your child can locate the capital C in the text on page 16.

Many children like to add their own creative touches to the Craft Sheets. If the crafts don't turn out how you expected, that's fine!

Remember, the important thing isn't the end product, but that your child interacts with the Letter of the Day.

Have your child do the ABC Craft Sheet for capital letter C.

Choose one or more activities from page 195 and complete them with your child.

Language Exploration

Play "Get Out of the Wagon!"

Take out the Wagon Sheet and the Picture Cards for Lesson 3 from your Activity Box. Make sure your child understands what each picture represents.

bat   hat   men   pen   bee   tree

house   mouse   king   ring   snail   jail

The Language Exploration section of each lesson features an activity or game that encourages phonological awareness, a Big Five Skill™.

The first eleven lessons include rhyming activities. Then we move on to games that explore syllables, initial sounds, word length, and more.

1. Lay three Picture Cards in the wagon at a time, two of which rhyme and one that does not.

2. Say the words aloud with your child.

3. Have your child identify the Picture Card that does not rhyme and take it out of the wagon, saying *Get out of the wagon!*

Read-Aloud Time

Read a Story or Poem

Read aloud to your child for twenty minutes.

Today when you are reading aloud, let your child hold the book as you read. Observe if your child understands how to hold the book the right side up (as opposed to upside down), and if the child knows to turn the pages in the correct direction.

Lesson 4 - Capital D

This lesson will teach capital letter D.

You will need: *My Book of Letters* page 13, Picture Cards for Lesson 4

Letter of the Day   Sing the Alphabet Song

Sing the Alphabet Song with your child. Point to the letters on the
Capital Letter Chart as each letter is named.

"Today's letter is D!" Have your child find the letter D
on the letter chart.

Complete Letter Activities for Capital D

Read the poem for the letter D on pages 19-22 of
The Zigzag Zebra.

See if your child can locate the capital D in the text on
page 20.

Have your child do the ABC Craft Sheet for capital
letter D.

Choose one or more activities from page 195 and
complete them with your child.

Language Exploration

Play "Rhyming Cards"

Take out the Picture Cards for Lesson 4 from your Activity Box. Make sure your child understands what each picture represents.

bell   shell   fan   van   hen   pen

train   rain   dog   log   phone   bone

"Remember that when words sound the same at the end, like *bell* and *shell*, they rhyme."

Mix up the Picture Cards. Lay them face up and have your child find the pairs that rhyme.

If your child needs extra help with this activity, use the following dialogue: **Tip!**

"Say this word with me: *bell*." *Bell.*

"Help me find the picture that rhymes with *bell*. -Ell, -ell, -ell. What sounds like -ell at the end?" *Child finds the* shell.

"Good! *Bell* and *shell* sound the same at the end, so they rhyme."

Read-Aloud Time

Read a Story or Poem

Read aloud to your child for twenty minutes.

The next time you are reading a picture book with only a sentence or two on a page, invite your child to count the number of words on the page with you. This helps your child understand that each grouping of letters is a word.

Lesson 5 - Capital E

This lesson will teach capital letter E and a new rhyming game.

You will need: *My Book of Letters* page 15, Picture Cards for Lesson 5

Letter of the Day   Sing the Alphabet Song

Sing the Alphabet Song with your child. Point to the letters on the Capital Letter Chart as each letter is named.

"Today's letter is E!" Have your child find the letter E on the letter chart.

Complete Letter Activities for Capital E

Read the poem for the letter E on pages 23-26 of *The Zigzag Zebra.*

Have your child do the ABC Craft Sheet for capital letter E.

Choose one or more activities from page 195 and complete them with your child.

Language Exploration

Play "Rhyming Concentration" with Ziggy

Take out the Picture Cards for Lesson 5 from your Activity Box. Make sure your child understands what each picture represents.

bell   shell   fan   van   hen   pen   train   rain

dog   log   phone   bone   mice   dice   snail   jail

The following rhyming activity is similar to the game of Concentration, except that the player must find two rhyming pictures (such as *dog* and *log*) rather than two identical pictures.

1. Shuffle the Picture Cards and lay them face down in a grid.

2. Take out the Ziggy Zebra puppet and put it on. Ziggy will play the game with your child.

Puppet: "Let's play a game together. We will take turns flipping the cards over two at a time. Then we have to say the words out loud to see if they rhyme. If the cards rhyme, whoever flipped them over gets to keep them. If they don't rhyme, we have to put them back on the table face down."

3. Continue the game until rhyming matches have been found for all cards.

4. Have Ziggy and your child count how many rhyming cards they found.

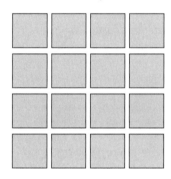

Tip!

If your child makes a mistake, have Ziggy make a similar mistake. Then have your child help you walk Ziggy through the process of finding rhyming cards.

Read-Aloud Time   Read a Story or Poem

Read aloud to your child for twenty minutes.

 Go beyond books! You don't have to wait for your special read-aloud time to read to your child, and you don't have to limit yourself to story books. Look around at every opportunity to see what else you can read.

Here are some ideas to show your child how fun and useful reading is—and that reading material can be found everywhere!

- When you plan a trip to the cinema, look up the show times in the newspaper. Once you get to the movie, point out the words that appear on the title screen, the introductory scroll that explains the history of what you are about to see, or the ending credits.
- Get a magazine subscription to a publication dedicated to one of your child's interests or hobbies.
- As you are cooking, read your recipes aloud as you put all the different ingredients together.
- At the doctor's office, you'll probably see plenty of signs giving instructions to the patients and posters with diagrams and words.
- While grocery shopping, read the signs over each aisle that tell you what items you can find there. Every product has labels, too, with tons of information to read.
- When you are putting together a bicycle, toy, or even a piece of furniture, read the instructions aloud as you go along.
- The next time your family goes to a restaurant, read the menu together.
- When traveling, read the traffic signs, business signs, billboards, and anything else you see along the way.

If you take every opportunity to read aloud to your child, he will soon learn that every part of our lives involves words!

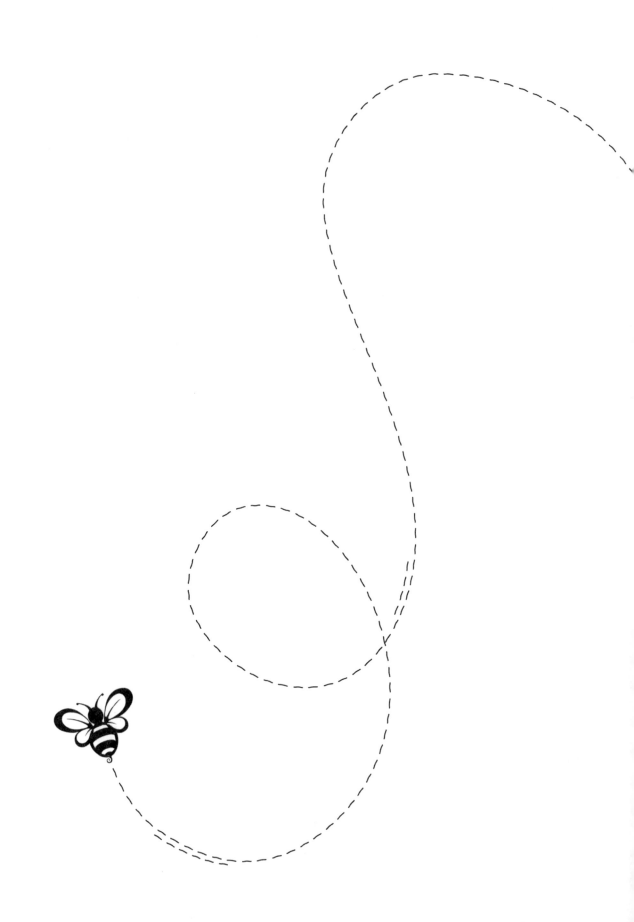

Lesson 6 - Capital F

This lesson will teach capital letter F.

You will need: *My Book of Letters* page 17, Picture Cards for Lesson 6, Wagon Sheet (*My Book of Letters* page 11)

Letter of the Day   Sing the Alphabet Song

Sing the Alphabet Song with your child. Point to the letters on the Capital Letter Chart as each letter is named.

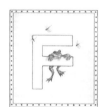

"Today's letter is F!" Have your child find the letter F on the letter chart.

Complete Letter Activities for Capital F

Read the poem for the letter F on pages 27-30 of *The Zigzag Zebra*.

See if your child can locate the capital F in the text on page 28.

Have your child do the ABC Craft Sheet for capital letter F.

Choose one or more activities from page 195 and complete them with your child.

Language Exploration

Play "Get Out of the Wagon!"

Take out the Wagon Sheet and the Picture Cards for Lesson 6 from your Activity Box. Make sure your child understands what each picture represents.

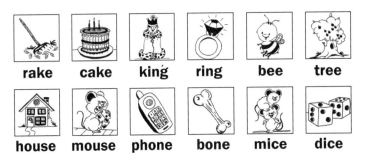

rake   cake   king   ring   bee   tree

house   mouse   phone   bone   mice   dice

1. Lay three Picture Cards in the wagon at a time, two of which rhyme and one that does not.

2. Say the words aloud with your child.

3. Have your child identify the Picture Card that does not rhyme and take it out of the wagon, saying *Get out of the wagon!*

Read-Aloud Time # Read a Story or Poem

Read aloud to your child for twenty minutes.

Lesson 7 - Capital G

This lesson will teach capital letter G and a new rhyming game.

You will need: *My Book of Letters* page 19

Letter of the Day   Sing the Alphabet Song

Sing the Alphabet Song with your child. Point to the letters on the Capital Letter Chart as each letter is named.

"Today's letter is G!" Have your child find the letter G on the letter chart.

Complete Letter Activities for Capital G

Read the poem for the letter G on pages 31-34 of *The Zigzag Zebra*.

See if your child can locate the capital G in the text on page 32.

Have your child do the ABC Craft Sheet for capital letter G.

Choose one or more activities from page 195 and complete them with your child.

Play "Stand Up or Sit Down"

Sit on the floor with your child.

"I will say two words. If these two words rhyme, stand up. If they don't rhyme, stay sitting."

"Day, play." *Child stands up.*

"Very good! *Day* and *play* **do** rhyme! Let's try some more."

Continue the game using the following pairs. Randomly intersperse non-rhyming pairs with rhyming pairs.

<u>**Rhyming pairs:**</u>	<u>**Non-rhyming pairs:**</u>
mad – sad	ball – ride
bear – chair	shoe – wet
see – three	ice – toy
bed – fed	cat – fun
ride – side	head – stop
kid – hid	hill – man
snow – low	
boy – joy	
how – now	
glue – blue	
cub – tub	

Read a Story or Poem

Read aloud to your child for twenty minutes.

 Introduce a new book by reading the title, author, and illustrator. Often, there is information about the author and illustrator included on the back flap or back cover.

A child's interest can be piqued when he realizes that an actual person wrote the book. For example, your child may be interested to learn that Beatrix Potter illustrated her own stories. Knowing the author's name can lead to questions like, "I wonder if this person wrote any other good books?"

Lesson 7: Capital G

Lesson 8 - Capital H

This lesson will teach capital letter H and a new rhyming game.

You will need: *My Book of Letters* page 21

Letter of the Day   Sing the Alphabet Song

Sing the Alphabet Song with your child. Point to the letters on the Capital Letter Chart as each letter is named.

"Today's letter is H!" Have your child find the letter H on the letter chart.

Complete Letter Activities for Capital H

Read the poem for the letter H on pages 35-38 of *The Zigzag Zebra*.

See if your child can locate the capital H in the text on pages 37 and 38.

Have your child do the ABC Craft Sheet for capital letter H.

Choose one or more activities from page 195 and complete them with your child.

Language Exploration

Play "Forgetful Zebra Rhyming Game" with Ziggy

Take out the Ziggy Zebra puppet and put it on.

Puppet: "I am a very forgetful zebra. I'm going to say some sentences that are missing a rhyming word at the end. Can you help me remember the rhymes and finish the sentences?"

Using Ziggy Zebra, read several of the rhyming sentences below and prompt your child to fill in the last word. Emphasize the bold rhyming word in each sentence.

"Look at the purple **bunny**! Doesn't he look _____?" *Funny.*

"On sunny days my **cat**... wears a wide-brimmed _____." *Hat.*

"If I had my **wish**, I'd catch a great big _____." *Fish.*

"I looked under the **rug**. I saw a cute little _____." *Bug.*

"I took a closer **look**. A worm was reading a _____!" *Book.*

"He's a very noisy **mouse**. He wakes everyone in the _____." *House.*

"At camp we had a **scare**. There was a big brown _____!" *Bear.*

"Did you see the **king**? He always wears a diamond _____." *Ring.*

"Off to the woods we **went**... to sleep in our new _____." *Tent.*

"What will we need to **buy**... to bake an apple _____?" *Pie.*

"Her dog's name is **Sticks**. He can do lots of _____." *Tricks.*

"I like to skip and **run**, and play outside in the _____." *Sun.*

Read-Aloud Time   Read a Story or Poem

Read aloud to your child for twenty minutes.

Lesson 8: Capital H

Lesson 9 - Capital I

This lesson will teach capital letter I and a new rhyming game.

You will need: *My Book of Letters* page 23, household items (see page 36)

Letter of the Day   Sing the Alphabet Song

Sing the Alphabet Song with your child. Point to the letters on the Capital Letter Chart as each letter is named.

"Today's letter is I!" Have your child find the letter I on the letter chart.

Complete Letter Activities for Capital I

Read the poem for the letter I on pages 39-42 of *The Zigzag Zebra*.

See if your child can locate the capital I in the text on page 40.

Have your child do the ABC Craft Sheet for capital letter I.

Choose one or more activities from page 195 and complete them with your child.

| **Language Exploration** | **Play "What's In My Bag?"** |

 For this game, you will need a bag and some household objects. Some suggestions are:

| spoon | pen | sock | book | cup |
| doll | key | shoe | pan | car |

Put all of the items in the bag.

"We're going to play another rhyming game. You will pull items out of my bag and tell me the name of the item. Then you have to say a word that rhymes with it. The word can be a real word or a nonsense word. If you pull out a pen, for example, you could say *hen* or a silly word like *nen*!"

Continue the game until your child has thought of rhyming words for every object.

Read-Aloud Time   **Read a Story or Poem**

Read aloud to your child for twenty minutes.

Lesson 10 - Capital J

This lesson will teach capital letter J and a new rhyming game.

You will need: *My Book of Letters* page 25, one of your child's favorite books

Letter of the Day   Sing the Alphabet Song

Sing the Alphabet Song with your child. Point to the letters on the Capital Letter Chart as each letter is named.

"Today's letter is J!" Have your child find the letter J on the letter chart.

Complete Letter Activities for Capital J

Read the poem for the letter J on pages 43-46 of *The Zigzag Zebra*.

See if your child can locate the capital J in the text on page 46.

Have your child do the ABC Craft Sheet for capital letter J.

Choose one or more activities from page 195 and complete them with your child.

Language Exploration

Read a Book with Ziggy

Take out one of your child's favorite story books and the Ziggy Zebra puppet.

As in the "Rhyming Body Parts" game in Lesson 1, Ziggy Zebra keeps saying the wrong word, so it's up to your child to tell him the right word. For this game, the correct word will rhyme with Ziggy's wrong word.

Puppet: "I'd like to play a game with you, but I keep saying the wrong words! Will you help me find the right rhyming words again?"

Take out your child's story book and begin the game with the dialogue below. The desired responses for your child are in italics.

"Let's read a **look** together." *You mean a book!*
"Yes, and I'll let you turn the **wages**." *You mean the pages!*
"Of course! I can't tell you how much I like to **deed**." *You mean read!*
"Right! What a smart **toy [curl]** you are!" *You mean boy [girl]!*

Continue this activity by having Ziggy Zebra actually read the book with your child. Every now and then, have Ziggy substitute one of the words in the book with a rhyming word. Your child can then tell Ziggy what the correct word should be.

Read-Aloud Time

Read a Story or Poem

Read aloud to your child for twenty minutes.

Believe it or not, some children think that you read the pictures, not the words on the page. Whether your child has this misconception or not, you should occasionally run your finger under the words as your read. Doing so reinforces the fact that you read from left to right and from top to bottom.

Lesson 11 - Capital K

This lesson will teach capital letter K and a new sentence game.

You will need: *My Book of Letters* pages 27 and 29

Letter of the Day

Sing the Alphabet Song

Sing the Alphabet Song with your child. Point to the letters on the Capital Letter Chart as each letter is named.

"Today's letter is K!" Have your child find the letter K on the letter chart.

Complete Letter Activities for Capital K

Read the poem for the letter K on pages 47-50 of *The Zigzag Zebra.*

Have your child do the ABC Craft Sheet for capital letter K.

Choose one or more activities from page 195 and complete them with your child.

Play "Name the Animals" with Ziggy

Take out the Jungle Sheet.

"Ziggy went to the jungle and met some new friends. Since they are wild animals, they don't have names. Ziggy wants to give them rhyming names. Can you help Ziggy think of some names?"

1. Encourage your child to come up with silly names for the animals. The names can be nonsense words, as long as they rhyme with the animal.

    Here are some examples to help you along: Jarret the Parrot, Liger the Tiger, Snaff the Giraffe, Ryan the Lion, Skunky the Monkey

2. As your child names the animals, write the names on the Jungle Sheet.

3. Post the Jungle Sheet on the refrigerator or send it to a relative.

Read a Story or Poem

Read aloud to your child for twenty minutes.

 Why do children like hearing the same story over and over?

Young children enjoy anticipating what comes next. They feel a sense of accomplishment when they know what's about to happen, get excited when their favorite part comes up, and feel satisfied when the book ends in the same predictable way. Children also focus on different parts of the story in subsequent readings. In the first reading, they may focus on what the characters are doing. In the second, they may focus on the events, and then on setting, story theme, humor, or minor characters.

Use this to your child's advantage. Your child may be able to recite part of the story from memory. If the story contains predictable text or rhymes, your child may also be able to finish the sentences.

Lesson 12 - Capital L

This lesson will teach capital letter L.

You will need: *My Book of Letters* page 31

Letter of the Day   Sing the Alphabet Song

Sing the Alphabet Song with your child. Point to the letters on the Capital Letter Chart as each letter is named.

"Today's letter is L!" Have your child find the letter L on the letter chart.

Complete Letter Activities for Capital L

Read the poem for the letter L on pages 51-54 of *The Zigzag Zebra*.

See if your child can locate two capital L's in the text on page 52.

Have your child do the ABC Craft Sheet for capital letter L.

Choose one or more activities from page 195 and complete them with your child.

Language Exploration

Play "Which Sentence Is Longer?" with Ziggy

Take out *The Zigzag Zebra* book and the Ziggy Zebra puppet. Begin this activity with the puppet so your child understands what he is being asked to do.

Turn to page 48. "I will say two sentences. See if you can tell which sentence is longer."

Hold up one finger to indicate sentence #1: "This is Kip."
Hold up two fingers to indicate sentence #2: "Kip is a baby kangaroo who rides in his mother's pouch."

 **Puppet:** "The second sentence is longer!"

Repeat this activity using the sentences below. Once your child understands the concept, have him respond instead of Ziggy.

Page:	Sentences:
8	"The crab runs away from the alligator." "The snake slithers."
18	"Here are three cats." "These calico cats love cookies and candy."
25	"The big elephant is afraid of the mouse." "The mouse is small."
28	"Four frogs are sitting on their lilypads." "Will they fall off?"
38	"This hippo is dirty." "The hippo makes a huge splash when she takes a bath!"
41	"These inchworms are tiny." "But they have to wear a lot of mittens when they ski!"

Read-Aloud Time

Read a Story or Poem

Read aloud to your child for twenty minutes.

Lesson 12: Capital L

Lesson 13 - Capital M

This lesson will teach capital letter M and a new sentence segmenting game.

You will need: *My Book of Letters* page 33, five small toys

Letter of the Day   Sing the Alphabet Song

Sing the Alphabet Song with your child. Point to the letters on the Capital Letter Chart as each letter is named.

"Today's letter is M!" Have your child find the letter M on the letter chart.

Complete Letter Activities for Capital M

Read the poem for the letter M on pages 55-58 of *The Zigzag Zebra*.

See if your child can locate the capital M in the text on page 56.

Have your child do the ABC Craft Sheet for capital letter M.

Choose one or more activities from page 195 and complete them with your child.

Play "Count the Words" with Ziggy

Before starting this activity, take out five small toys like wooden blocks or toy cars.

During the game, be sure your child sets down the toys from left to right to reinforce correct directionality.

Take out the Ziggy Zebra puppet and put it on.

"Let's play a game called 'Count the Words.' First I'll say a sentence, and then Ziggy will repeat it. Ziggy will set down a toy for each word I say, and then he will count the toys. For example, the first sentence is *I like books*. Watch what Ziggy does now."

This activity leads your child to understand that sentences can be broken up (*segmented*) into individual words. This is the most basic segmenting activity, and future segmenting activities will build on it.

Progressively more advanced games in future lessons will guide your child in segmenting words into syllables and segmenting syllables into phonemes (individual sounds).

Repeat the sentence slowly with clear pauses between each word. Have the puppet set down a toy for each word and then count the toys.

"Now it's your turn."

Continue this activity using the sentences below, which contain two or three words. Have Ziggy encourage and help your child throughout the game.

Dogs bark.
Frank drank milk.
They laughed.
Draw a horse.
Sit down.
Goats are cute!

Now try the following sentences, which contain more than three words. If your child is ready, say the sentences with normal speed. Do not pause between the words. When your child repeats the sentence back to you and Ziggy, the child can pause between words as he sets down the toy.

Some children hesitate to count the words *the* or *a* as "real" words. You can assure them that these words do indeed count.

My cat is fat.
Pam has eight ducks.
I ate an egg.
Who is in the barn?
She lost her shoe.
Where is your nose?

Lesson 13: Capital M

Read-Aloud Time   Read a Story or Poem

Read aloud to your child for twenty minutes.

It can be an interesting adventure to visit sites that you are reading about. Local places to visit in relation to a story can include the park, library, police station, fire station, hospital, vet, lake or pond, candy store, or book store. Look around your community to find areas that relate to the story and can bring it more to life.

Some destinations or activities require a half day or even a full day to experience. Ideas include the zoo, a natural history museum, an art museum, local historic sites, holiday events, historical reenactments, a play, a fishing trip, or boating.

Other places that are too far away could become part of a family vacation. These sites might include battlefields, the home of Laura Ingalls Wilder, the state capital, and national historic sites.

One of the advantages of books is that they can take you places you cannot ordinarily go, so don't feel pressured to take field trips to every place your read-alouds mention. But if there is an easy correlation between a favorite book and an actual location, it can be worth the trip.

Lesson 14 - Capital N

This lesson will teach capital letter N and a new word blending game.

You will need: *My Book of Letters* page 35

Letter of the Day   Sing the Alphabet Song

Sing the Alphabet Song with your child. Point to the letters on the Capital Letter Chart as each letter is named.

"Today's letter is N!" Have your child find the letter N on the letter chart.

"N stands for *nanny goat!*"

Complete Letter Activities for Capital N

Read the poem for the letter N on pages 59-62 of *The Zigzag Zebra.*

Have your child do the ABC Craft Sheet for capital letter N.

Choose one or more activities from page 195 and complete them with your child.

Language Exploration

Play "Guess the Word" #1

"Now we're going to play 'Guess the Word.' I will say a word in two parts, and you will figure out what the word is."

"Here's the first one: *sun...shine*. Can you figure out the word?" *Sunshine.*

"Good! Let's do some more."

When saying the compound words in this activity, pause between the two parts of the words.

You say:	Your child says:
"Foot...ball."	*Football.*
"Cob...web."	*Cobweb.*
"Shoe...box."	*Shoebox.*
"Scare...crow."	*Scarecrow.*
"Air...plane."	*Airplane.*
"Tea...spoon."	*Teaspoon.*
"Inch...worm."	*Inchworm.*
"Cup...cake."	*Cupcake.*
"Nut...shell."	*Nutshell.*
"Rail...road."	*Railroad.*

This game introduces the concept of blending. Learning to blend syllables is an important part of decoding (reading).

Read-Aloud Time   Read a Story or Poem

Read aloud to your child for twenty minutes.

Lesson 14: Capital N

Lesson 15 - Capital O

This lesson will teach capital letter O.

You will need: *My Book of Letters* page 37

Letter of the Day   Sing the Alphabet Song

Sing the Alphabet Song with your child. Point to the letters on the Capital Letter Chart as each letter is named.

"Today's letter is O!" Have your child find the letter O on the letter chart.

Complete Letter Activities for Capital O

Read the poem for the letter O on pages 63-66 of *The Zigzag Zebra*.

Have your child do the ABC Craft Sheet for capital letter O.

Choose one or more activities from page 195 and complete them with your child.

Play "Guess the Word" #2 with Ziggy

Take out the Ziggy Zebra puppet and put it on.

Puppet: "I'm going to say a word in a funny way. You will try to guess the word."

"Here's the first one: *lit...tle*. Can you figure out the word?" *Little.*

"Very good! Let's do some more."

When saying the words in this activity, have Ziggy pause between the two syllables.

Ziggy says:	Your child says:
"Hap...py."	*Happy.*
"Pump...kin."	*Pumpkin.*
"Rock...et."	*Rocket.*
"Pan...ther."	*Panther.*
"Chick...en."	*Chicken.*
"Mar...ble."	*Marble.*
"Trum...pet."	*Trumpet.*
"Sham...poo."	*Shampoo.*
"Li...zard."	*Lizard.*
"Sur...prise."	*Surprise.*

After your child is successful with two-syllable words, try the following three-syllable words. However, if your child is not ready for three-syllable words, come back to this activity another day.

Ziggy says:	Your child says:
"Di...no...saur."	*Dinosaur.*
"Te...le...phone."	*Telephone.*
"Le...mo...nade."	*Lemonade.*
"Bi...cy...cle."	*Bicycle.*
"Ex...er...cise."	*Exercise.*
"To...ma...to."	*Tomato.*
"Se...ven...teen."	*Seventeen.*
"La...dy...bug."	*Ladybug.*
"Alph...a...bet."	*Alphabet.*
"Por...cu...pine."	*Porcupine.*

Read-Aloud Time   Read a Story or Poem

Read aloud to your child for twenty minutes.

 Here is a simple way to tell if your child has developed print awareness, one of the Big Five Skills™. Give your child a book and ask him or her to show you:

- the front of the book
- the title of the book
- the first page of the book
- a letter
- the first word on the page
- how to turn the page
- where to find the page number
- the last page of the book
- the back cover

Don't be concerned if your child can't identify these items. Just be aware that you should casually bring up these topics during your read-aloud times. Reassess your child in a month.

Lesson 16 - Capital P

This lesson will teach capital letter P.

You will need: *My Book of Letters* page 39, five small toys

Letter of the Day   Sing the Alphabet Song

Sing the Alphabet Song with your child. Point to the letters on the Capital Letter Chart as each letter is named.

"Today's letter is P!" Have your child find the letter P on the letter chart.

Complete Letter Activities for Capital P

Read the poem for the letter P on pages 67-60 of *The Zigzag Zebra*.

Have your child do the ABC Craft Sheet for capital letter P.

Choose one or more activities from page 195 and complete them with your child.

Language Exploration

Play "Count the Words" with Ziggy

Before starting this activity, take out five small toys like wooden blocks or toy cars.

During the game, be sure your child sets down the toys from left to right to reinforce correct directionality.

Take out the Ziggy Zebra puppet and put it on.

 **Puppet**: "Let's play 'Count the Words' again! First I'll say a sentence, and then I'll repeat it. I will set down a toy for each word I say, and then I will count the toys. For example, my first sentence is *Frogs jump high*. Watch what I do now."

Ziggy repeats the sentence slowly with clear pauses between each word. Have the puppet set down a toy for each word and then count the toys.

"Now it's your turn!"

Continue this activity using the sentences below, which contain two or three words. Have Ziggy encourage and help your child throughout the game.

> **Sam played.**
> **Bees can sting.**
> **We ate.**
> **Sing a song.**
> **Be good.**
> **Mice are small.**

Now try the following sentences, which contain more than three words. This time, say the sentences with normal speed. Do not pause between the words. When your child repeats the sentence back to you and Ziggy, the child can pause between words as he sets down the toy.

Some children hesitate to count the words *the* or *a* as "real" words. You can assure them that these words do indeed count.

> **Hop on one leg.**
> **I found a dime.**
> **Bats stay up all night.**
> **You have two eyes.**
> **She counts to ten.**
> **My hog wears a hat.**

Lesson 16: Capital P

Read-Aloud Time   Read a Story or Poem

Read aloud to your child for twenty minutes.

Do you have a wiggly child? Some kids get uncomfortable if they are made to sit still—their little legs and arms and bodies just want to go, go, go! If you have one of these children, you know what I mean. You try to get them to sit on your lap for a read-aloud, and they stiffen and slide right off!

Read-alouds are still important for wiggly kids, but some accommodations have to be made. Don't make wigglers sit perfectly still while you are reading aloud or they will grow to dislike reading time. You can let them draw quietly with crayons, knead Fimo clay or modeling wax, or build with LEGO® bricks. If they can keep their hands busy, it is easier for them to stay in one place and pay attention to what you are reading.

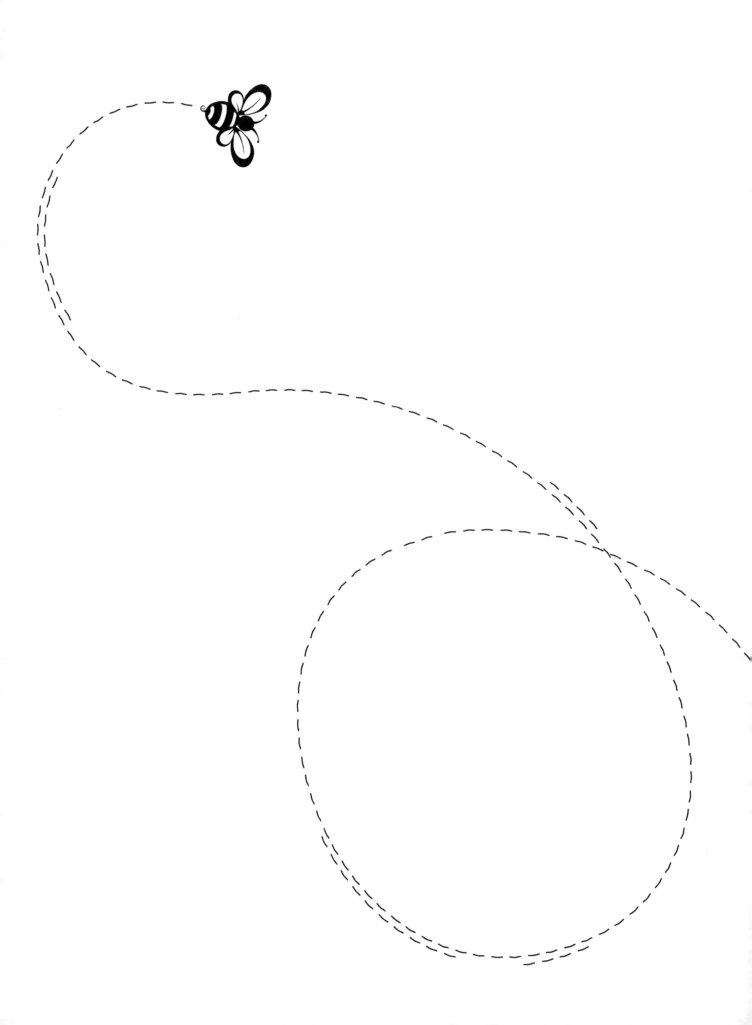

Lesson 17 - Capital Q

This lesson will teach capital letter Q and a new syllable segmenting game.

You will need: *My Book of Letters* page 41

Letter of the Day   Sing the Alphabet Song

Sing the Alphabet Song with your child. Point to the letters on the Capital Letter Chart as each letter is named.

"Today's letter is Q!" Have your child find the letter Q on the letter chart.

"What sound do ducks make?" *Quack*.

"Right! Q stands for *quack*!"

Complete Letter Activities for Capital Q

Read the poem for the letter Q on pages 71-74 of *The Zigzag Zebra*.

See if your child can locate the capital Q in the text on page 72.

Have your child do the ABC Craft Sheet for capital letter Q.

Choose one or more activities from page 195 and complete them with your child.

Language Exploration

Play "Clap Your Name"

"We are going to play 'Clap Your Name.' Since your name is [Michael], we will clap it like this: *Mi* [clap hands]...*chael* [clap hands]. Now you try it with me." *Child claps his name.*

"Very good! Now let's clap the names of our family members. Let's start with [name of family member]. Ready?"

Continue the game by clapping the syllables in the names of family, friends, and neighbors. You can include both first and last names.

"The word parts we've been clapping out are called *syllables*."

> This game introduces the concept of syllables. As your child learns to recognize syllables, he is paying attention to different parts of the words, which will help him when it comes to reading and spelling.
>
> Some children don't grasp the concept behind "Clap Your Name" on the first day they play it. That's okay! There are more variations of this game coming up in future lessons, so your child will have other opportunities to practice this skill.

Read-Aloud Time

Read a Story or Poem

Read aloud to your child for twenty minutes.

> If you're reading a story in which words are repeated, have your child participate in the telling. Simply stop reading and let your child fill in the repeated word or phrase. You may want to add these books with predictable text to your reading list:
>
> *Brown Bear, Brown Bear, What Do You See?* by Bill Martin, Jr.
> *The Wheels on the Bus* by Raffi
> *Are You My Mother?* by P.D. Eastman
> *Over in the Meadow* by Ezra Jack Keats
> *Have You Seen My Duckling?* by Nancy Tafuri
> *The Three Billy Goats Gruff* by Ellen Appleby
> *The Very Hungry Caterpillar* by Eric Carle

Lesson 18 - Capital R

This lesson will teach capital letter R and a new syllable segmenting game.

You will need: *My Book of Letters* page 43

Letter of the Day   Sing the Alphabet Song

Sing the Alphabet Song with your child. Point to the letters on the Capital Letter Chart as each letter is named.

"Today's letter is R!" Have your child find the letter R on the letter chart.

Complete Letter Activities for Capital R

Read the poem for the letter R on pages 75-78 of *The Zigzag Zebra.*

Have your child do the ABC Craft Sheet for capital letter R.

Choose one or more activities from page 195 and complete them with your child.

<table>
<tr><td>

Language Exploration

</td><td>

Play "Clap the Syllables" #1 with Ziggy

</td></tr>
</table>

In this activity, your child will repeat two-syllable words and clap his hands on each syllable. For example:

Airplane: *Air* [clap hands]—*plane* [clap hands]

Trophy: *Tro* [clap hands]—*phy* [clap hands]

Take out the Ziggy Zebra puppet and put it on.

Puppet: "Today we are going to play 'Clap the Syllables.' I will say a word, and you will repeat the word and clap your hands for every syllable. Let's try one: *toolbox*." *Child repeats the word and claps his hands on each syllable: tool [clap hands]—box [clap hands].*

"Good! Let's do some more."

Continue the game with Ziggy, using the following words:

barefoot	**turkey**	**shuttle**
farmer	**giraffe**	**monster**
cartwheel	**windy**	**snowflake**
stopwatch	**jaybird**	**water**
armchair	**peaches**	**silly**

Your child might enjoy one of these variations of the game: have your child jump for each syllable, or tap out the syllables with rhythm sticks, a triangle, or other small instrument.

Tip!

Read-Aloud Time   Read a Story or Poem

Read aloud to your child for twenty minutes.

Lesson 18: Capital R

Lesson 19 - Capital S

This lesson will teach capital letter S.

You will need: *My Book of Letters* page 45

Letter of the Day   Sing the Alphabet Song

Sing the Alphabet Song with your child. Point to the letters on the
Capital Letter Chart as each letter is named.

 "Today's letter is S!" Have your child find the letter S
on the letter chart.

Complete Letter Activities for Capital S

 Read the poem for the letter S on pages 79-82 of
The Zigzag Zebra.

 Have your child do the ABC Craft Sheet for capital
letter S.

 Choose one or more activities from page 195 and
complete them with your child.

Play "Clap the Syllables" #2 with Ziggy

In this activity, your child will repeat three-syllable words and clap his hands on each syllable. For example:

Department: *De* [clap hands]—*part* [clap hands]—*ment* [clap hands]

Overboard: *O* [clap hands]—*ver* [clap hands]—*board* [clap hands]

If your child is unable to clap the syllables, set the syllable games aside for now. Come back to them in a month or two and try again.

Tip!

Puppet: "You did such a good job with the 'Clap the Syllables' game we played the last time. Now we can play it with bigger words! I will say a word, and you will repeat the word and clap your hands for every syllable. Let's try one: *elephant.*" *Child repeats the word and claps his hands on each syllable:*
el [clap hands]—*e* [clap hands]—*phant* [clap hands].

"Good! Let's do some more."

Continue the game with Ziggy, using the following words:

afternoon	family	acrobat
licorice	octopus	sunnier
animal	horizon	terrible
calendar	jellyfish	tiniest
butterscotch	radio	fantastic

Read-Aloud Time   Read a Story or Poem

Read aloud to your child for twenty minutes.

Before re-reading a favorite book, pretend you don't remember the story. Ask your child, "What happens to Goldilocks?" Remembering and retelling the story helps your child's verbal development and encourages him to become an active listener.

Lesson 20 - Capital T

This lesson will teach capital letter T and a new word length game.

You will need: *My Book of Letters* page 47

Letter of the Day Sing the Alphabet Song

Sing the Alphabet Song with your child. Point to the letters on the Capital Letter Chart as each letter is named.

"Today's letter is T!" Have your child find the letter T on the letter chart.

Complete Letter Activities for Capital T

Read the poem for the letter T on pages 83-86 of *The Zigzag Zebra*.

See if your child can locate the capital T in the text on pages 84 and 86.

Have your child do the ABC Craft Sheet for capital letter T.

Choose one or more activities from page 195 and complete them with your child.

Language Exploration

Play "Which Word Is Longer?"

"I will say two words. See if you can tell which word is longer: *butter*, *butterfly*." *Butterfly*.

"Good! Let's try some more."

Continue the game with the following words.

You say:	Your child says:
"Ant, elephant."	*Elephant.*
"Milk, mushroom."	*Mushroom.*
"Umbrella, wet."	*Umbrella.*
"Kangaroo, jump."	*Kangaroo.*
"Grass, bumblebee."	*Bumblebee.*
"Tree, bluebird."	*Bluebird.*
"Jellyfish, sand."	*Jellyfish.*

This activity encourages your child to listen for the different sounds in a word. The ability to do this will help your child learn to read and spell more easily.

Read-Aloud Time

Read a Story or Poem

Read aloud to your child for twenty minutes.

 Read aloud to your child as often as you can—more than once a day if possible. Keep a book handy for when you have ten minutes before leaving for an appointment or fifteen minutes while dinner is cooking. If you keep a book in your purse or bag, you'll have one ready when you're in the dentist's waiting room or if you arrive someplace early.

Lesson 21 - Capital U

This lesson will teach capital letter U and a new word segmenting game.

You will need: *My Book of Letters* page 49

Letter of the Day   Sing the Alphabet Song

Sing the Alphabet Song with your child. Point to the letters on the Capital Letter Chart as each letter is named.

"Today's letter is U!" Have your child find the letter U on the letter chart.

Complete Letter Activities for Capital U

Read the poem for the letter U on pages 87-90 of *The Zigzag Zebra*.

Have your child do the ABC Craft Sheet for capital letter U.

Choose one or more activities from page 195 and complete them with your child.

Language Exploration	## Play "Cooperation" with Ziggy

 Take out the Ziggy Zebra puppet and put it on. In this game, your child will be segmenting the first sound of a word.

"I will say the beginning of a word, and Ziggy will say the rest of the word. See if you can guess the word."

Teacher: "Sss..."
Puppet: "...lipper."

"Can you guess the word?" *Slipper.*

"Good! Let's try another one."

Teacher: "Mmm..."
Puppet: "...ap."
Child: *Map.*

Continue the game with the following words.

> Remember, you are saying the first *sound* in the word, rather than the name of the letter. Then Ziggy is finishing the word.

You say:	Ziggy says:	Your child says:
"Fff..."	"...unny."	*Funny.*
"Lll..."	"...amp."	*Lamp.*
"Mmm..."	"...other."	*Mother.*
"Nnn..."	"...oisy."	*Noisy.*
"Fff..."	"...amily."	*Family.*
"Rrr..."	"...abbit."	*Rabbit.*

Read-Aloud Time	## Read a Story or Poem

Read aloud to your child for twenty minutes.

Lesson 22 - Capital V

This lesson will teach capital letter V and a new syllable segmenting game.

You will need: *My Book of Letters* pages 51 and 53, Picture Cards for Lesson 22

Letter of the Day

Sing the Alphabet Song

Sing the Alphabet Song with your child. Point to the letters on the Capital Letter Chart as each letter is named.

"Today's letter is V!" Have your child find the letter V on the letter chart.

Complete Letter Activities for Capital V

Read the poem for the letter V on pages 91-94 of *The Zigzag Zebra*.

See if your child can locate the capital V in the text on page 92.

Have your child do the ABC Craft Sheet for capital letter V.

Choose one or more activities from page 195 and complete them with your child.

| **Language Exploration** | **Play "Hop To It"** |

Take out the Animal Tracks Sheet and cut along the dotted lines to form three pieces of paper.

Take out the Picture Cards for Lesson 22 from your Activity Box. Make sure your child understands what each picture represents.

apple   flag   igloo   crab   monkey   octopus

queen   umbrella   violin   underwear   worm   zipper

Shuffle the Picture Cards and put them in a pile. Lay the Animal Tracks Sheets numbered 1, 2, and 3 on the floor.

Many children will still need to clap out the syllables as they did in Lessons 18 and 19.

Tip!

"Today we are going to play 'Hop To It.' You will pick a Picture Card from this pile and tell me the word of the picture you see. Let's try one." *Child picks a card and says the word.*

"Good! Now count how many syllables the word has. If it has one syllable, hop on the number 1. If it has two syllables, hop on the number 2. If it has three syllables, hop on the number 3. How many syllables does this word have?" *Child responds and hops on the corresponding number sheet.*

Continue the game until the child has done all twelve Picture Cards correctly.

Read-Aloud Time   Read a Story or Poem

Read aloud to your child for twenty minutes.

Lesson 23 - Capital W

This lesson will teach capital letter W.

You will need: *My Book of Letters* page 55

Letter of the Day   Sing the Alphabet Song

Sing the Alphabet Song with your child. Point to the letters on the Capital Letter Chart as each letter is named.

"Today's letter is W!" Have your child find the letter W on the letter chart.

Complete Letter Activities for Capital W

Read the poem for the letter W on pages 95-98 of *The Zigzag Zebra*.

Have your child do the ABC Craft Sheet for capital letter W.

Choose one or more activities from page 195 and complete them with your child.

Language Exploration

Play "Cooperation" with Ziggy

Puppet: "You did such a good job of guessing words the other day, we're going to play the guessing game again. Your teacher will say the beginning of a word, and I will say the rest of the word. See if you can guess the word."

Teacher: "Fff..."
Puppet: "...lag!"

"Can you guess the word?" *Flag.*

"Good! Let's try some more."

Continue the game with the following words.

You say:	Ziggy says:	Your child says:
"Fff..."	"...rog."	*Frog.*
"Sss..."	"...unny."	*Sunny.*
"Nnn..."	"...est."	*Nest.*
"Lll..."	"...eaves."	*Leaves.*
"Sss..."	"...tar."	*Star.*
"Mmm..."	"...ice."	*Mice.*

> Remember, you are saying the first *sound* in the word, rather than the name of the letter. Then Ziggy is finishing the word.

Read-Aloud Time

Read a Story or Poem

Read aloud to your child for twenty minutes.

> One of the main benefits of reading aloud is that doing so improves the child's background knowledge. The child learns about many different cultures, places, and animals. Through books, the child experiences things that he couldn't otherwise experience. He can learn about ancient cultures and beliefs, how things work, and what space travel is like. Effortlessly, the child gains information that will aid his comprehension when he begins to read on his own.

Lesson 24 - Capital X

This lesson will teach capital letter X and a new word segmenting game.

You will need: *My Book of Letters* page 57

Letter of the Day   Sing the Alphabet Song

Sing the Alphabet Song with your child. Point to the letters on the Capital Letter Chart as each letter is named.

"Today's letter is X!" Have your child find the letter X on the letter chart.

Complete Letter Activities for Capital X

Read the poem for the letter X on pages 99-102 of *The Zigzag Zebra*.

Have your child do the ABC Craft Sheet for capital letter X.

Choose one or more activities from page 195 and complete them with your child.

Language Exploration

Play "Copycat" with Ziggy

"Ziggy and I are going to play a game called 'Copycat.' I will say a word, and Ziggy will repeat the end of the word."

Teacher: "Mouse."
Puppet: "...ouse."
Teacher: "Car."
Puppet: "...ar."

"Now it's your turn. I'll say a word, and you'll say the end of the word, just like Ziggy did."

Continue the game with the words below. Have Ziggy help and encourage your child during the game.

You say:	Your child says:
"Day."	...ay.
"Bake."	...ake.
"Leaf."	...eaf.
"Pull."	...ull.
"Wheel."	...eel.
"Beak."	...eak.
"Goose."	...oose.
"Rain."	...ain.
"Head."	...ead.
"Cow."	...ow.

Read-Aloud Time Read a Story or Poem

Read aloud to your child for twenty minutes.

Lesson 25 - Capital Y

This lesson will teach capital letter Y and a new word segmenting game.

You will need: *My Book of Letters* page 59

Letter of the Day   Sing the Alphabet Song

Sing the Alphabet Song with your child. Point to the letters on the Capital Letter Chart as each letter is named.

"Today's letter is Y!" Have your child find the letter Y on the letter chart.

Complete Letter Activities for Capital Y

Read the poem for the letter Y on pages 103-106 of *The Zigzag Zebra*.

Have your child do the ABC Craft Sheet for capital letter Y.

Choose one or more activities from page 195 and complete them with your child.

Play "Story Time" with Ziggy

"Ziggy wants to tell us a story. Listen carefully. If he says any words wrong, you can help him say the right word."

Exaggerate Ziggy's incorrect words. Your child's desired responses are shown in italics.

Puppet: "Last night I couldn't **-leep**." *You mean* sleep*!*
Teacher: "What sound did Ziggy leave out?" *Sss.*

Continue this pattern for the rest of the short story below. Each time, the child should say the sound that Ziggy leaves out.

"Last night I had a terrible **-oothache**." *You mean* toothache*!*

"It hurt so much, all my **-tripes** fell off." *You mean* stripes*!*

"I swept my stripes up with a **-room**." *You mean* broom*!*

"And I stuck them back on with **-lue**." *You mean* glue*!*

"It was a big job that took me all **-ight**." *You mean* night*!*

"But I forgot all about my sore **-ooth**!" *You mean* tooth*!*

Read a Story or Poem

Read aloud to your child for twenty minutes.

Active readers make predictions about what is going to happen next in a story. And making predictions is a big part of reading comprehension, because it stems from understanding what just happened.

When you are reading aloud, encourage this habit by occasionally stopping to ask, "What do you think will happen next?" By doing so, you'll know if your child has been listening and if he understands what has happened up to this point in the story.

Lesson 26 - Capital Z

This lesson will teach capital letter Z and a new word blending game.

You will need: *My Book of Letters* pages 61 and 63, Picture Cards for Lesson 26, yarn or string

Letter of the Day   Sing the Alphabet Song

Sing the Alphabet Song with your child. Point to the letters on the Capital Letter Chart as each letter is named.

"Today's letter is Z!" Have your child find the letter Z on the letter chart.

Complete Letter Activities for Capital Z

Read the poem for the letter Z on pages 107-110 of *The Zigzag Zebra*.

Have your child do the ABC Craft Sheet for capital letter Z.

Choose one or more activities from page 195 and complete them with your child.

Play "Snail Talk" with Ziggy

Before beginning this lesson, attach string or yarn to the Snail Sheet to make a necklace.

Take out the Picture Cards for Lesson 26 from your Activity Box. Make sure your child understands what each picture represents.

alligator   ant   apple   bed   flag   glove   goose   horse

Put the Picture Cards in a pile.

Take out the Ziggy Zebra puppet and put the snail necklace on him.

Puppet: "We are going to play a game called 'Snail Talk.' Snails move very, very slowly, and if they could talk, I imagine they would talk very slowly, too!"

"I'll be the snail first. I will pick a card from the pile and say the word very slowly, like a snail. Then you will say the word at regular speed."

Have Ziggy draw a Picture Card from the pile and say the word slowly. For example, if Ziggy draws the *ant* card, he says *aaannnt*. Your child should repeat the word at regular speed: *ant*.

Go through all of the cards once, and then put the snail necklace on your child. Go through the cards again, this time with the child drawing the Picture Cards and saying the words very slowly.

> The ability to blend is critical to your child's reading success. When your child begins to read, he will sound out individual sounds, often in a disconnected manner. Oral blending activities will help him develop the skill of forming a word out of isolated sounds.
>
> In the "Snail Talk" game, the sounds are said slowly, but they are still slightly connected. In future blending games, the sounds will be disconnected from each other.

Read-Aloud Time   Read a Story or Poem

Read aloud to your child for twenty minutes.

Part 2
Lowercase Letters

Tips for Part 2 (Lessons 27–52)

- **Switch to the Lowercase Letter Chart.** For easy access, display it on the wall, the refrigerator, or the back of a door.

- **Keep the *Lizard Lou* book handy.** You'll be reading a short selection from this book each day. The illustrations in *Lizard Lou* emphasize the most common sound of each alphabet letter. This is the sound that your child will need to know when beginning to read. *Lizard Lou* includes components that promote all of the Big Five Skills™.

- **VERY IMPORTANT: Be sure you understand what slashes on both sides of a letter mean.** Take a look at this example from the facing page:

  > Read the poems for the letter <u>a</u> on pages 7-10 of *Lizard Lou*. Point out the drawings and mention the items that start with the letter <u>a</u>:
  >   "/ă/.../ă/...*apple* starts with <u>a</u>."
  >   "/ă/.../ă/...*animal* crackers. *Animal* starts with <u>a</u>."
  >   "/ă/.../ă/...*ant* starts with <u>a</u>."

You'll notice that the letter <u>a</u> is surrounded by slashes and has a mark over it. This means that you should say the short sound of the letter <u>a</u>, not the name of the letter.

To hear pronunciations of each of the letter sounds, refer to the CD-ROM called *Letter Sounds A to Z*.

Lesson 27 - Lowercase A

This lesson will teach lowercase letter <u>a</u>.

You will need: *My Book of Letters* pages 65 and 67

Letter of the Day   Sing the Alphabet Song

Sing the Alphabet Song with your child. Point to the letters on the Lowercase Letter Chart as each letter is named.

"Today's letter is <u>a</u>!" Have your child find the letter <u>a</u> on the letter chart.

Complete Letter Activities for Lowercase A

Refer to the last tip on page 78 for an explanation of the slash marks.

Read the poems for the letter <u>a</u> on pages 7-10 of *Lizard Lou*. Point out the drawings and mention the items that start with the letter <u>a</u>:
"/ă/.../ă/...*apple* starts with <u>a</u>."
"/ă/.../ă/...*animal* crackers. *Animal* starts with <u>a</u>."
"/ă/.../ă/...*ant* starts with <u>a</u>."

Have your child do the ABC Craft Sheet for lowercase letter <u>a</u>. Ask your child, "What letter does *apple* start with?"

Letter of the Day

(continued)

Choose one or more activities from page 195 and complete them with your child.

Have your child complete the sheet "Circle the <u>a</u>."

The letter <u>a</u> has two basic shapes: ***a*** and <u>a</u>. The first shape is most commonly used in handwriting and informal fonts. The second shape, <u>a</u>, is used in most text.

Use your judgment as to whether it is a good time to introduce this sheet to your child. You can use this sheet today or save it until your child is ready.

These letters also have two basic shapes: <u>g</u>, <u>q</u>, <u>t</u>, <u>y</u>.

Language Exploration

Play "Story Time" with Ziggy

"Ziggy wants to tell us another story. Listen carefully. If he says any words wrong, you can help him say the right word."

Exaggerate Ziggy's incorrect words. Your child's desired responses are shown in italics.

Puppet: "One time I met a ferocious **-iger**." *You mean tiger!*
Teacher: "What sound did Ziggy leave out?" */t/.*

Continue this pattern for the rest of the short story below. Each time, the child should say the sound that Ziggy leaves out.

"Instead of chasing me, he just sat on the **-round**." *You mean* ground*!*

"I asked him why he was sad, and he started to **-ry**." *You mean* cry*!*

"He said he didn't like to chase **-ebras** like me." *You mean* zebras*!*

"And the other tigers laughed and made **-un** of him." *You mean* fun*!*

"He preferred to eat green leaves and pretty **-lowers**." *You mean* flowers*!*

"So I took him home to my **-amily**." *You mean* family*!*

"And he's happy to graze in the **-arden** with us." *You mean* garden*!*

In this game, your child is learning to isolate the beginning sound of a word.

Read-Aloud Time   Read a Story or Poem

Read aloud to your child for twenty minutes.

 If you pick a book that you loved from your own childhood, chances are your child will catch your enthusiasm for the story.

Do you remember any of these books?

The Runaway Bunny by Margaret Wise Brown
Blueberries for Sal by Robert McCloskey
Make Way for Ducklings by Robert McCloskey
Caps for Sale by Esphyr Slobodkina
The Complete Adventures of Curious George by H.A. Rey
Corduroy by Don Freeman
My Cat Likes to Hide in Boxes by Eve Sutton
Lyle, Lyle, Crocodile by Bernard Waber
Madeline by Ludwig Bemelmans
The Story of Ferdinand by Munro Leaf

Lesson 28 - Lowercase B

This lesson will teach lowercase letter b.

You will need: *My Book of Letters* page 69

Letter of the Day

Sing the Alphabet Song

Sing the Alphabet Song with your child. Point to the letters on the Lowercase Letter Chart as each letter is named.

"Today's letter is b!" Have your child find the letter b on the letter chart.

Complete Letter Activities for Lowercase B

When you point out the drawings and repeat the initial sound of each item, your child will hear the sounds that the individual letters make.

At this point, we aren't asking your chid to remember the sounds or recite them back—but we are providing exposure to the big idea that letters make specific sounds.

Read the poems for the letter b on pages 11-14 of *Lizard Lou*. Point out the drawings and mention the items that start with the letter b:
  "/b/.../b/...*bird* starts with b."
  "/b/.../b/...*boy* starts with b."
  "/b/.../b/...*bat* starts with b."

Have your child do the ABC Craft Sheet for lowercase letter b. Ask your child, "What letter does *bat* start with?"

Choose one or more activities from page 195 and complete them with your child.

**Language
Exploration**

Play "Which Word Is Longer?"

"I will say two words. See if you can tell which word is longer: *box, beetle.*" *Beetle.*

"Good! Let's try some more."

Continue the game with the following words.

You say:	Your child says:
"Bird, dandelion."	*Dandelion.*
"Sailboat, sky."	*Sailboat.*
"Radio, toy."	*Radio.*
"Hop, jackrabbit."	*Jackrabbit.*
"Pillow, doll."	*Pillow.*
"Cup, water."	*Water.*
"Dragonfly, yard."	*Dragonfly.*

Read-Aloud Time

Read a Story or Poem

Read aloud to your child for twenty minutes.

 Let your child see you reading. For example, when you read for your own pleasure, be sure to sit someplace where your child can see you.

Here are some other ways to demonstrate that reading is enjoyable and useful:

- When you prepare a recipe, read the list of ingredients and instructions aloud.
- Spread out the newspaper and announce that you are going to read.
- When you read silently, choose funny or interesting parts to read aloud or talk about.

Lesson 29 - Lowercase C

This lesson will teach lowercase letter c and a new word blending game.

You will need: *My Book of Letters* page 71

Letter of the Day   Sing the Alphabet Song

Sing the Alphabet Song with your child. Point to the letters on the Lowercase Letter Chart as each letter is named.

"Today's letter is c!" Have your child find the letter c on the letter chart.

Complete Letter Activities for Lowercase C

Read the poems for the letter c on pages 15-18 of *Lizard Lou*. Point out the drawings and mention the items that start with the letter c:
>   "/k/.../k/...*crow* starts with c."
>   "/k/.../k/...*cow* starts with c."
>   "/k/.../k/...*crocodile* starts with c."

Have your child do the ABC Craft Sheet for lowercase letter c. Ask your child, "What letter does *cow* start with?"

Choose one or more activities from page 195 and complete them with your child.

Play "Put It Together" with Ziggy

Take out the Ziggy Zebra puppet and put it on.

Puppet: "I only like to say whole words, but I have a bunch of words that are in parts. I will say the words in parts, and you will help me put them back together. Let's try one."

"The word I want to put together is *p…an*. Do you know what the word is?" *Pan!*

"Right! Let's do some more."

Ziggy says:	Your child says:
"T…ub."	*Tub.*
"F…ast."	*Fast.*
"S…ack."	*Sack.*
"R…un."	*Run.*
"H…elp."	*Help.*
"N…ote."	*Note.*
"J…ar."	*Jar.*
"Y…ell."	*Yell.*
"B…urp."	*Burp.*
"W…et."	*Wet.*
"C…an."	*Can.*

Read-Aloud Time   Read a Story or Poem

Read aloud to your child for twenty minutes.

Lesson 30 - Lowercase D

This lesson will teach lowercase letter d.

You will need: *My Book of Letters* page 73

Letter of the Day   Sing the Alphabet Song

Sing the Alphabet Song with your child. Point to the letters on the Lowercase Letter Chart as each letter is named.

"Today's letter is d!" Have your child find the letter d on the letter chart.

Complete Letter Activities for Lowercase D

Read the poems for the letter d on pages 19-22 of *Lizard Lou*. Point out the drawings and mention the items that start with the letter d:
>"/d/.../d/...*deer* starts with d."
>"/d/.../d/...*donkey* starts with d."
>"/d/.../d/...*dandelion* starts with d."

Have your child do the ABC Craft Sheet for lowercase letter d. Ask your child, "What letter does *deer* start with?"

Choose one or more activities from page 195 and complete them with your child.

Play "Copycat" with Ziggy

"Ziggy and I are going to play 'Copycat' again. I will say a word, and Ziggy will repeat the end of the word."

Teacher: "Bug."
Puppet: "...ug."
Teacher: "Wheat."
Puppet: "...eat."

"Now it's your turn. I'll say a word, and you'll say the end of the word, just like Ziggy did."

Continue the game with the words below. Have Ziggy help and encourage your child during the game.

You say:	Your child says:
"Zoo."	...oo.
"Light."	...ight.
"Wood."	...ood.
"Back."	...ack.
"How."	...ow.
"March."	...arch.
"Weight."	...eight.
"Horn."	...orn.
"Lock."	...ock.
"Wig."	...ig.

Read-Aloud Time   Read a Story or Poem

Read aloud to your child for twenty minutes.

Lesson 31 - Lowercase E

This lesson will teach lowercase letter e and a new word blending game.

You will need: *My Book of Letters* page 75

Letter of the Day   Sing the Alphabet Song

Sing the Alphabet Song with your child. Point to the letters on the Lowercase Letter Chart as each letter is named.

"Today's letter is e!" Have your child find the letter e on the letter chart.

Complete Letter Activities for Lowercase E

Read the poems for the letter e on pages 23-26 of *Lizard Lou*. Point out the drawings and mention the items that start with the letter e:
"/ĕ/ .../ĕ/ ...echo starts with e."
"/ĕ/ .../ĕ/ ...elephant starts with e."
"/ĕ/ .../ĕ/ ...eggs starts with e."

Have your child do the ABC Craft Sheet for lowercase letter e. Ask your child, "What letter does *echo* start with?"

Choose one or more activities from page 195 and complete them with your child.

Language Exploration

Play "Guess the Animal"

"I am going to say the names of the animals on a farm. I will say the words in parts, and you will guess what the animal is."

You say:	Your child says:
"H…orse."	*Horse.*
"D…uck."	*Duck.*
"P…ig."	*Pig.*
"Ch…icken."	*Chicken.*
"G…oat."	*Goat.*
"C…ow."	*Cow.*
"H…en."	*Hen.*
"M…ule."	*Mule.*
"Sh…eep."	*Sheep.*
"R…ooster."	*Rooster.*
"T…urkey."	*Turkey.*
"L…amb."	*Lamb.*

Read-Aloud Time

Read a Story or Poem

Read aloud to your child for twenty minutes.

 Build your own library of books. The more books you have at home, the more opportunities your child has to pick one up and read.

Besides the books your child receives as gifts, check out these places for affordable books for your library: rummage sales, library book sales, resale shops, clearance racks at book stores, and online places like swap.com.

Lesson 32 - Lowercase F

This lesson will teach lowercase letter f and a new word blending game.

You will need: *My Book of Letters* page 77, Picture Cards for Lesson 32

Letter of the Day   Sing the Alphabet Song

Sing the Alphabet Song with your child. Point to the letters on the Lowercase Letter Chart as each letter is named.

"Today's letter is f!" Have your child find the letter f on the letter chart.

Complete Letter Activities for Lowercase F

Read the poems for the letter f on pages 27-30 of *Lizard Lou*. Point out the drawings and mention the items that start with the letter f:
   "/f/.../f/...*firefly* starts with f."
   "/f/.../f/...*fish* starts with f."
   "/f/.../f/...*flowers* starts with f."

Have your child do the ABC Craft Sheet for lowercase letter f. Ask your child, "What letter does *fish* start with?"

Choose one or more activities from page 195 and complete them with your child.

Language Exploration

Play "I Spy" with Ziggy

Take out the Picture Cards for Lesson 32 from your Activity Box.
Make sure your child understands what each picture represents.

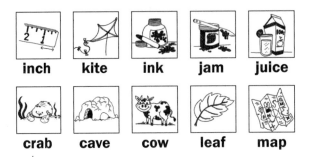

inch   kite   ink   jam   juice

crab   cave   cow   leaf   map

Place the Picture Cards around the room. Take out the Ziggy Zebra
puppet and put it on.

Puppet: "Today we will play 'I Spy.' I will look around
the room for pictures and tell you the name of the
picture one sound at a time. Then you will tell me what
the picture is. Let's try one."

"I spy with my little zebra eye a l...ea...f. Do you know what I'm looking
at?" *Leaf!*

"Right! Let's do some more. I spy with my little zebra eye..."

Ziggy says:	Your child says:
a c...r...a...b."	*Crab.*
a k...i...te."	*Kite.*
some j...ui...ce."	*Juice.*
a m...a...p."	*Map.*
a c...a...ve."	*Cave.*
an i...n...ch."	*Inch.*
some j...a...m."	*Jam.*
some i...nk."	*Ink.*
a c...o...w."	*Cow.*

Read-Aloud Time   Read a Story or Poem

Read aloud to your child for twenty minutes.

Lesson 32: Lowercase F

Lesson 33 - Lowercase G

This lesson will teach lowercase letter g and a new initial sounds game.

You will need: *My Book of Letters* pages 79, 81, and 83, Picture Cards for Lesson 33

Letter of the Day   Sing the Alphabet Song

Sing the Alphabet Song with your child. Point to the letters on the Lowercase Letter Chart as each letter is named.

"Today's letter is g!" Have your child find the letter g on the letter chart.

Complete Letter Activities for Lowercase G

Read the poems for the letter g on pages 31-34 of *Lizard Lou*. Point out the drawings and mention the items that start with the letter g:
> "/g/.../g/...*goose* starts with g."
> "/g/.../g/...*garden* starts with g."
> "/g/.../g/...*girl* starts with g."

Have your child do the ABC Craft Sheet for lowercase letter g. Ask your child, "What letter does *goose* start with?"

Choose one or more activities from page 195 and complete them with your child.

Letter of the Day
(continued)

Have your child complete the sheet "Circle the g."

The letter g has two basic shapes: g and g. The first shape is most commonly used in handwriting and informal fonts. The second shape, g, is used in most text.

Use your judgment as to whether it is a good time to introduce this sheet to your child. You can use this sheet today or save it until your child is ready.

Language Exploration

Play "Ziggy Takes a Trip"

Take out the Backpack Sheet and the Picture Cards for Lesson 33 from your Activity Box. Make sure your child understands what each picture represents.

Spread out the Picture Cards around the Backpack Sheet.

Puppet: "I am going on a trip to see my dear Aunt Suzie, and I need to pack interesting things to show her. I only want to take things that start with the sound of /s/. Will you help me pack?"

Language Exploration
(continued)

Have your child help Ziggy choose the items that start with the sound of /s/ and put them on top of the Backpack Sheet. If Ziggy puts the wrong item in the backpack, the child should correct him.

Read-Aloud Time   Read a Story or Poem

Read aloud to your child for twenty minutes.

To keep your child's interest high, look for nonfiction books related to your child's specific interests and hobbies. You can also stimulate new interests by choosing read-alouds on topics that are completely new to your child.

Here are some topics that are popular with children:

airplanes	ecosystems	pets
ancient Egypt	farm animals	planets
baby animals	fossils	plants
birds	holidays around the world	rain forests
boats	horses	recipes for children
cars	human body	snakes
crafts	insects	space exploration
dinosaurs	jokes	trains
dolphins	other countries	the Wild West

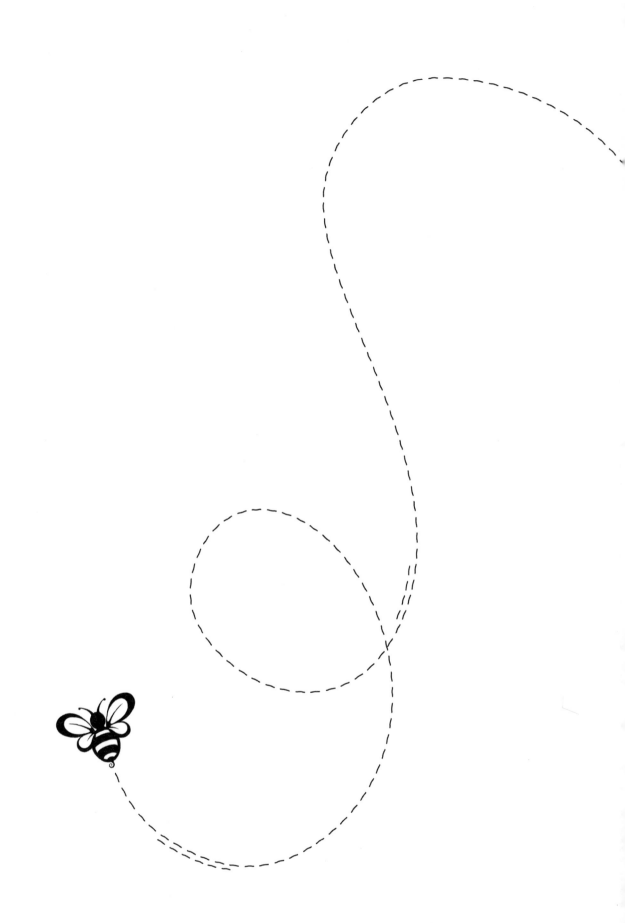

Lesson 34 - Lowercase H

This lesson will teach lowercase letter <u>h</u>.

You will need: *My Book of Letters* page 85, Picture Cards for Lesson 34, Backpack Sheet (*My Book of Letters* page 83)

Letter of the Day

Sing the Alphabet Song

Sing the Alphabet Song with your child. Point to the letters on the Lowercase Letter Chart as each letter is named.

"Today's letter is <u>h</u>!" Have your child find the letter <u>h</u> on the letter chart.

Complete Letter Activities for Lowercase H

Read the poems for the letter <u>h</u> on pages 35-38 of *Lizard Lou*. Point out the drawings and mention the items that start with the letter <u>h</u>:
"/h/.../h/...*hat* starts with <u>h</u>."
"/h/.../h/...*horn* starts with <u>h</u>."
"/h/.../h/...*horse* starts with <u>h</u>."

Have your child do the ABC Craft Sheet for lowercase letter <u>h</u>. Ask your child, "What letter does *hat* start with?"

Choose one or more activities from page 195 and complete them with your child.

Language Exploration

Play "Ziggy Takes a Trip"

Take out the Backpack Sheet and the Picture Cards for Lesson 34 from your Activity Box. Make sure your child understands what each picture represents.

log   lion   bell   leaf   monkey

lock   pumpkin   lips   toad   vacuum

Spread out the Picture Cards around the Backpack Sheet.

Puppet: "I am going on another trip! This time I will visit my cousin Larry, and I want to show him interesting things that start with the sound of /l/. Will you help me pack again?"

Have your child help Ziggy choose the items that start with the sound of /l/ and put them on top of the Backpack Sheet. If Ziggy puts the wrong item in the backpack, the child should correct him.

Read-Aloud Time

Read a Story or Poem

Read aloud to your child for twenty minutes.

As you read a story, ask your child why a character acts a certain way. For example, if you are reading *Goldilocks and the Three Bears*, ask why Goldilocks tastes the porridge from all three bowls. If reading Aesop's fables, ask why the fox gave up trying to get the grapes. And if reading the stories of Peter Rabbit, ask why Peter disobeyed or why his mother warned him not to get into any trouble.

Lesson 35 - Lowercase I

This lesson will teach lowercase letter i.

You will need: *My Book of Letters* page 87, Picture Cards for Lesson 35,

Wagon Sheet (*My Book of Letters* page 11)

Letter of the Day   Sing the Alphabet Song

Sing the Alphabet Song with your child. Point to the letters on the Lowercase Letter Chart as each letter is named.

"Today's letter is i!" Have your child find the letter i on the letter chart.

Complete Letter Activities for Lowercase I

Read the poems for the letter i on pages 39-42 of *Lizard Lou*. Point out the drawings and mention the items that start with the letter i:
    "/ĭ/.../ĭ/...*itchy* starts with i."
    "/ĭ/.../ĭ/...*igloo* starts with i."
    "/ĭ/.../ĭ/...*insect* starts with i."

Have your child do the ABC Craft Sheet for lowercase letter i. Ask your child, "What letter does *itchy* start with?"

Choose one or more activities from page 195 and complete them with your child.

Language Exploration

Play "Get Out of the Wagon!"

Take out the Wagon Sheet and the Picture Cards for Lesson 35 from your Activity Box. Make sure your child understands what each picture represents.

fan   flag   map   monkey   nail   net

rat   road   vacuum   violin   zebra   zipper

> The last time your child played "Get Out of the Wagon!", rhyming words were emphasized. This time, we are concentrating on the sound at the beginning of the word.

1. Lay three Picture Cards in the wagon at a time, two of which begin with the same sound and one that begins with a different sound.

2. Say the words aloud with your child.

3. Have your child identify the Picture Card that does not begin with the same sound as the others and take it out of the wagon, saying *Get out of the wagon!*

Read-Aloud Time

Read a Story or Poem

Read aloud to your child for twenty minutes.

> Plan a special time of day to read to your child, such as before naptime, after lunch, or as part of the bedtime ritual. If your schedule is too full to fit in twenty minutes of daily reading, look at what you can cut out. At this stage of your child's life, hearing good books is more important than most other enrichment activities.

Lesson 36 - Lowercase J

This lesson will teach lowercase letter j.

You will need: *My Book of Letters* page 89, Picture Cards for Lesson 36, Wagon Sheet (*My Book of Letters* page 11)

Letter of the Day Sing the Alphabet Song

Sing the Alphabet Song with your child. Point to the letters on the Lowercase Letter Chart as each letter is named.

"Today's letter is j!" Have your child find the letter j on the letter chart.

Complete Letter Activities for Lowercase J

Read the poems for the letter j on pages 43-46 of *Lizard Lou*. Point out the drawings and mention the items that start with the letter j:
> "/j/.../j/...*jam* starts with j."
> "/j/.../j/...*jacket* starts with j."
> "/j/.../j/...*jewels* starts with j."

Have your child do the ABC Craft Sheet for lowercase letter j. Ask your child, "What letter does *jam* start with?"

Choose one or more activities from page 195 and complete them with your child.

Language Exploration

Play "Get Out of the Wagon!"

Take out the Wagon Sheet and the Picture Cards for Lesson 36 from your Activity Box. Make sure your child understands what each picture represents.

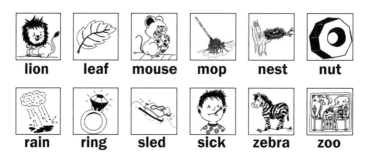

1. Lay three Picture Cards in the wagon at a time, two of which begin with the same sound and one that begins with a different sound.

2. Say the words aloud with your child.

3. Have your child identify the Picture Card that does not begin with the same sound as the others and take it out of the wagon, saying *Get out of the wagon!*

Read-Aloud Time

Read a Story or Poem

Read aloud to your child for twenty minutes.

 While you are reading, take the time to enjoy and talk about the illustrations. You can have your child point out favorite characters, objects, and colors, or ask him why the artist drew something a certain way.

Once you are done reading, let your child create his own piece of art inspired by the story.

Lesson 37 - Lowercase K

This lesson will teach lowercase letter k and a new initial sounds game.

You will need: *My Book of Letters* page 91

Letter of the Day   Sing the Alphabet Song

Sing the Alphabet Song with your child. Point to the letters on the Lowercase Letter Chart as each letter is named.

"Today's letter is k!" Have your child find the letter k on the letter chart.

Complete Letter Activities for Lowercase K

Read the poems for the letter k on pages 47-50 of *Lizard Lou*. Point out the drawings and mention the items that start with the letter k:
"/k/.../k/...*key* starts with k."
"/k/.../k/...*kite* starts with k."
"/k/.../k/...*kitten* starts with k."

Have your child do the ABC Craft Sheet for lowercase letter k. Ask your child, "What letter does *kite* start with?"

Choose one or more activities from page 195 and complete them with your child.

Language Exploration

Play "Silly Sentences" with Ziggy

In this activity, each word in the sentence begins with a sound that is easy to hold. Have Ziggy exaggerate the sounds in the first few examples.

"Ziggy and I are going to play 'Silly Sentences.' I am going to say a sentence, and Ziggy will listen carefully: *Mary might make muffins.* What sound does each word start with?"

Show Ziggy going through the proper thought process.

Puppet: "Hmm...Mmmary mmmight mmmake mmmuffins. Each word starts with *mmm!*"

"Very good! Let's try some more."

Continue the activity using the sentences below. Once your child understands what to do, have him identify the first sound of the words instead of Ziggy.

You have probably noticed that some sounds are easier to hold than others. Sibilant sounds—those that are easy to hold—are easier for children to identify as well. Sibilant sounds include the vowel sounds and /f/, /l/, /m/, /n/, /r/, /s/, /v/, and /z/.

You say:	Ziggy/your child says:
"Fred found five fish."	*Fff.*
"Robert rubs red rocks."	*Rrr.*
"Vicky viewed velvet vests."	*Vvv.*
"Sam sewed seven socks."	*Sss.*
"Nancy never needs naps."	*Nnn.*
"Larry's lizard laughed."	*Lll.*

Read-Aloud Time   Read a Story or Poem

Read aloud to your child for twenty minutes.

Lesson 37: Lowercase K

Lesson 38 - Lowercase L

This lesson will teach lowercase letter l.

You will need: *My Book of Letters* page 93

Letter of the Day   Sing the Alphabet Song

Sing the Alphabet Song with your child. Point to the letters on the Lowercase Letter Chart as each letter is named.

"Today's letter is l!" Have your child find the letter l on the letter chart.

Complete Letter Activities for Lowercase L

Read the poems for the letter l on pages 51-54 of *Lizard Lou*. Point out the drawings and mention the items that start with the letter l:
> "/l/.../l/...*lion* starts with l."
> "/l/.../l/...*lizard* starts with l."
> "/l/.../l/...*lollipop* starts with l."

Have your child do the ABC Craft Sheet for lowercase letter l. Ask your child, "What letter does *leaf* start with?"

Choose one or more activities from page 195 and complete them with your child.

Play "Silly Sentences" with Ziggy

In this activity, each word in the sentence begins with a sound that is easy to hold. Have Ziggy encourage your child to repeat the sentences, exaggerating the initial sounds.

"You did such a good job with the 'Silly Sentences' game that Ziggy wants to play it again. Ziggy will say a sentence. You will listen carefully and say which sound each word starts with."

Puppet: "Here is the first sentence: *Nobody knows Nan's neice.* What sound does each word start with?"
Child: *Nnnobody knnows Nnnan's nnniece. Nnn.*
Puppet: "Very good! Let's try some more."

Continue the activity using the sentences below.

Ziggy says:	Your child says:
"Miss Maple made maps."	*Mmm.*
"Sing silly songs."	*Sss.*
"Let lions lick lollipops."	*Lll.*
"Funny frogs float."	*Fff.*
"Ron's rabbits ran races."	*Rrr.*
"Zesty zebras zoom."	*Zzz.*

Read-Aloud Time   Read a Story or Poem

Read aloud to your child for twenty minutes.

You can enhance your child's experience of a story by using visual aids before, during, or after reading.

Anything that is in the story will do, such as foods, colors, stuffed animals, plants, musical instruments—even brothers and sisters!

Lesson 39 - Lowercase M

This lesson will teach lowercase letter <u>m</u>.

You will need: *My Book of Letters* page 95, Picture Cards for Lesson 39,

Backpack Sheet (*My Book of Letters* page 83)

Letter of the Day   Sing the Alphabet Song

Sing the Alphabet Song with your child. Point to the letters on the Lowercase Letter Chart as each letter is named.

"Today's letter is <u>m</u>!" Have your child find the letter <u>m</u> on the letter chart.

Complete Letter Activities for Lowercase M

Read the poems for the letter <u>m</u> on pages 55-58 of *Lizard Lou*. Point out the drawings and mention the items that start with the letter <u>m</u>:

"/m/.../m/...*moon* starts with <u>m</u>."
"/m/.../m/...*mouse* starts with <u>m</u>."
"/m/.../m/...*mirror* starts with <u>m</u>."

Have your child do the ABC Craft Sheet for lowercase letter <u>m</u>. Ask your child, "What letter does *moon* start with?"

Choose one or more activities from page 195 and complete them with your child.

Language Exploration

Play "Ziggy Takes a Trip"

Take out the Backpack Sheet and the Picture Cards for Lesson 39 from your Activity Box. Make sure your child understands what each picture represents.

truck   bed   tree   jam

pig   tub   quilt   toad

Spread out the Picture Cards around the Backpack Sheet.

Puppet: "I am going on another trip! This time I will visit my friend Terry, and I want to show him interesting things that start with the sound of /t/. Will you help me pack again?"

Have your child help Ziggy choose the items that start with the sound of /t/ and put them on top of the Backpack Sheet. If Ziggy puts the wrong item in the backpack, the child should correct him.

Read-Aloud Time

Read a Story or Poem

Read aloud to your child for twenty minutes.

Lesson 39: Lowercase M

Lesson 40 - Lowercase N

This lesson will teach lowercase letter n.

You will need: *My Book of Letters* page 97, Picture Cards for Lesson 40,
Wagon Sheet (*My Book of Letters* page 11)

Letter of the Day   Sing the Alphabet Song

Sing the Alphabet Song with your child. Point to the letters on the
Lowercase Letter Chart as each letter is named.

"Today's letter is n!" Have your child find the letter n
on the letter chart.

Complete Letter Activities for Lowercase N

Read the poems for the letter n on pages 59-62 of
Lizard Lou. Point out the drawings and mention the
items that start with the letter n:
"/n/.../n/...*nest* starts with n."
"/n/.../n/...*nut* starts with n."
"/n/.../n/...*newt* starts with n."

Have your child do the ABC Craft Sheet for lowercase
letter n. Ask your child, "What letter does *nest* start
with?"

Choose one or more activities from page 195 and
complete them with your child.

Language Exploration

Play "Get Out of the Wagon!"

Take out the Wagon Sheet and the Picture Cards for Lesson 40 from your Activity Box. Make sure your child understands what each picture represents.

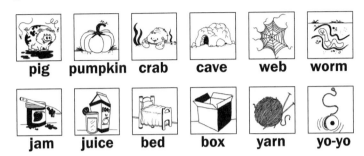

1. Lay three Picture Cards in the wagon at a time, two of which begin with the same sound and one that begins with a different sound.

2. Say the words aloud with your child.

3. Have your child identify the Picture Card that does not begin with the same sound as the others and take it out of the wagon, saying *Get out of the wagon!*

Read-Aloud Time

Read a Story or Poem

Read aloud to your child for twenty minutes.

Find out what resources your library offers. You may be able to take advantage of story time, summer reading programs, craft classes, puppet shows, or children's books on CD. Some libraries host "meet the author" events or invite local community members like firemen, dentists, police officers, and nurses.

Lesson 40: Lowercase N

Lesson 41 - Lowercase O

This lesson will teach lowercase letter o.

You will need: *My Book of Letters* page 99

Letter of the Day Sing the Alphabet Song

Sing the Alphabet Song with your child. Point to the letters on the Lowercase Letter Chart as each letter is named.

"Today's letter is o!" Have your child find the letter o on the letter chart.

Complete Letter Activities for Lowercase O

Read the poems for the letter o on pages 63-66 of *Lizard Lou*. Point out the drawings and mention the items that start with the letter o:
"/ŏ/ .../ŏ/ ...*otter* starts with o."
"/ŏ/ .../ŏ/ ...*ocelot* starts with o."
"/ŏ/ .../ŏ/ ...*ox* starts with o."

Have your child do the ABC Craft Sheet for lowercase letter o. Ask your child, "What letter does *otter* start with?"

Choose one or more activities from page 195 and complete them with your child.

Play "Silly Sentences" with Ziggy

In this activity, each word in the sentence begins with a "stop" sound—a sound that cannot be held. Have Ziggy repeat and exaggerate the sounds in the first few examples.

"Let's play 'Silly Sentences' again. I am going to say a sentence, and Ziggy will listen carefully: *Tod teased ten toads.* What sound does each word start with?"

Show Ziggy going through the proper thought process.

Puppet: "T...T...Tod t...t...teased t...t...ten t...t...toads. Each word starts with /t/!"

"Very good! Let's try some more."

Continue the activity using the sentences below. Once your child understands what to do, have him identify the first sound of the words instead of Ziggy.

Stop sounds can only be said for an instant, so they can be more difficult for children to identify than sibilant sounds.

Letters with stop sounds include <u>b</u>, <u>c</u>, <u>d</u>, g, j, <u>k</u>, p, q, <u>t</u>, and <u>x</u>.

You say:	Ziggy/your child says:
"Geese gobble grapes."	/g/.
"Did Deb dance?"	/d/.
"Purple pigs picked plums."	/p/.
"Wendy's wagon was white."	/w/.
"King Ken cooked crabs."	/k/.
"Bob blew bubbles."	/b/.

Read-Aloud Time   Read a Story or Poem

Read aloud to your child for twenty minutes.

Lesson 42 - Lowercase P

This lesson will teach lowercase letter p.

You will need: *My Book of Letters* page 101

Letter of the Day   Sing the Alphabet Song

Sing the Alphabet Song with your child. Point to the letters on the Lowercase Letter Chart as each letter is named.

"Today's letter is p!" Have your child find the letter p on the letter chart.

Complete Letter Activities for Lowercase P

Read the poems for the letter p on pages 67-70 of *Lizard Lou*. Point out the drawings and mention the items that start with the letter p:

"/p/.../p/...*pig* starts with p."
"/p/.../p/...*pine tree* starts with p."
"/p/.../p/...*policeman* starts with p."

Have your child do the ABC Craft Sheet for lowercase letter p. Ask your child, "What letter does *pig* start with?"

Choose one or more activities from page 195 and complete them with your child.

| **Language Exploration** | **Play "Silly Sentences" with Ziggy** |

In this activity, each word in the sentence begins with a "stop" sound—a sound that cannot be held. Have Ziggy encourage your child to repeat and exaggerate the initial sounds.

"You did such a good job with the 'Silly Sentences' game that Ziggy wants to play it again. Ziggy will say a sentence. You will listen carefully and say which sound each word starts with."

Puppet: "Here is the first sentence: *Buy brown boots.* What sound does each word start with?"
Child: *B...b...buy b...b...brown b...b...boots. They start with /b/!*
Puppet: "Very good! Let's try some more."

Continue the activity using the sentences below.

Ziggy says:	**Your child says:**
"Use yellow yarn."	/y/.
"Tammy told tall tales."	/t/.
"Do dogs dig ditches?"	/d/.
"Pam peeled pears."	/p/.
"Kim keeps quiet."	/k/.
"Jerry juggles juice jugs."	/j/.

Read-Aloud Time **Read a Story or Poem**

Read aloud to your child for twenty minutes.

You can enhance your read-aloud time by chatting with your child afterward. Discuss what the story was about, or just talk about any new words, sounds, or ideas your child discovered.

Lesson 43 - Lowercase Q

This lesson will teach lowercase letter q and a new final sound game.

You will need: *My Book of Letters* pages 103 and 105

Letter of the Day   Sing the Alphabet Song

Sing the Alphabet Song with your child. Point to the letters on the Lowercase Letter Chart as each letter is named.

"Today's letter is q!" Have your child find the letter q on the letter chart.

Complete Letter Activities for Lowercase Q

Read the poems for the letter q on pages 71-74 of *Lizard Lou*. Point out the drawings and mention the items that start with the letter q:

"/kw/.../kw/...*quack* starts with q."
"/kw/.../kw/...*queen* starts with q."
"/kw/.../kw/...*question mark* starts with q."

Have your child do the ABC Craft Sheet for lowercase letter q. Ask your child, "What letter does *queen* start with?"

Choose one or more activities from page 195 and complete them with your child.

Letter of the Day
(continued)

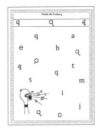

Have your child complete the sheet "Circle the q."

The letter q has two basic shapes: 𝑞 and q. The first shape is most commonly used in handwriting and informal fonts. The second shape, q, is used in most text.

Use your judgment as to whether it is a good time to introduce this sheet to your child. You can use this sheet today or save it until your child is ready.

Language Exploration

Play "Finish the Words" with Ziggy

"Ziggy wanted to play a game, but he bit his tongue and it hurts! Now when he tries to talk, he doesn't always say the last sound in the word. Let's see if you can figure out what Ziggy is trying to say."

Puppet: "I like to eat macaroni and chee..."
Child: *Macaroni and cheese!*
Teacher: "What sound did Ziggy leave out?"
Child: */z/.*

"Very good! Let's try another one."

Puppet: "Put my hotdog in a hotdog bu..."
Child: *Hotdog bun!*
Teacher: "What sound did Ziggy not say?"
Child: */n/.*

Continue the activity using the sentences on the following page.

In this activity, your child is learning to isolate and pay attention to the last sound in a word.

Lesson 43: Lowercase Q

Language Exploration
(continued)

Ziggy says:	Your child says:
"Please answer the telepho..."	Telephone.
"You need a lawnmower to mow the gra..."	Grass.
"I hear the ringing of the church be..."	Bell.
"My favorite pizza topping is pepperon..."	Pepperoni.
"I looked up to the sky and saw a falling sta..."	Star.
"Do you want to sail in a big boa...?"	Boat.

Read-Aloud Time Read a Story or Poem

Read aloud to your child for twenty minutes.

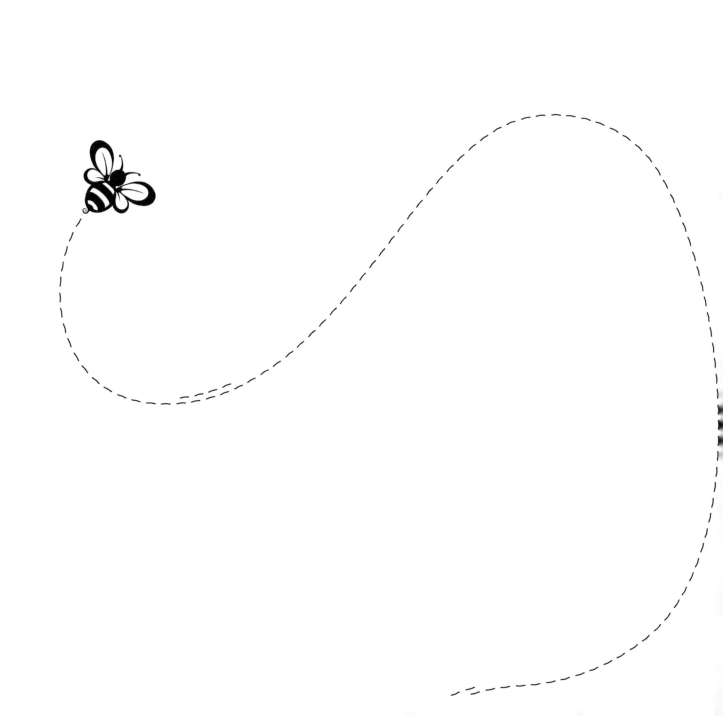

Lesson 44 - Lowercase R

This lesson will teach lowercase letter r.

You will need: *My Book of Letters* page 107

Letter of the Day   Sing the Alphabet Song

Sing the Alphabet Song with your child. Point to the letters on the Lowercase Letter Chart as each letter is named.

"Today's letter is r!" Have your child find the letter r on the letter chart.

Complete Letter Activities for Lowercase R

Read the poems for the letter r on pages 75-78 of *Lizard Lou*. Point out the drawings and mention the items that start with the letter r:
> "/r/.../r/...*rabbit* starts with r."
> "/r/.../r/...*rake* starts with r."
> "/r/.../r/...*rattlesnake* starts with r."

Have your child do the ABC Craft Sheet for lowercase letter r. Ask your child, "What letter does *rake* start with?"

Choose one or more activities from page 195 and complete them with your child.

Language Exploration	## Play "Finish the Words" with Ziggy

**Language
Exploration**

Play "Finish the Words" with Ziggy

"Ziggy's tongue is feeling a bit better today, but it is still sore and he can't finish his words. Let's see what words he is trying to say."

Puppet: "I like to wear a cowboy ha..."
Child: *Cowboy hat!*
Teacher: "What sound did Ziggy leave out?"
Child: */t/.*

"Very good! Let's help him some more."

Continue the activity using the sentences below.

<u>Ziggy says:</u>	<u>Your child says:</u>
"Please clean the rug with a vacuu..."	*Vacuum.*
"In the morning, I drink orange jui..."	*Juice.*
"I went to the zoo and saw a tall gira..."	*Giraffe.*
"The grass is as green as a string bea..."	*Bean.*
"My left hand is cold because I have only one winter glo..."	*Glove.*
"Let's sit down and read a good boo..."	*Book.*

Read-Aloud Time   Read a Story or Poem

Read aloud to your child for twenty minutes.

Lesson 45 - Lowercase S

This lesson will teach lowercase letter s̲.

You will need: *My Book of Letters* page 109

Letter of the Day   Sing the Alphabet Song

Sing the Alphabet Song with your child. Point to the letters on the Lowercase Letter Chart as each letter is named.

"Today's letter is s̲!" Have your child find the letter s̲ on the letter chart.

Complete Letter Activities for Lowercase S

Read the poems for the letter s̲ on pages 79-82 of *Lizard Lou*. Point out the drawings and mention the items that start with the letter s̲:

"/s/.../s/...*sun* and *squirrel* start with s̲."
"/s/.../s/...*scorpion* starts with s̲."
"/s/.../s/...*snowman* starts with s̲."

Have your child do the ABC Craft Sheet for lowercase letter s̲. Ask your child, "What letter does *sun* start with?"

Choose one or more activities from page 195 and complete them with your child.

Language Exploration	## Play "Finish the Words" with Ziggy

Language Exploration

Play "Finish the Words" with Ziggy

"I think Ziggy's tongue must be feeling better today. But he has developed a habit of not saying the last sound in the word. Can you help him?"

Puppet: "I rode on a choo choo trai..."
Child: *Choo choo train!*
Teacher: "What sound did Ziggy leave out?"
Child: */n/.*

"Very good! Let's help him some more."

Continue the activity using the sentences below.

Ziggy says:	Your child says:
"In the winter, we can build a snowma..."	*Snowman.*
"If you want something, it's best to say plea..."	*Please.*
"Did you ever swim in a swimming poo...?"	*Pool.*
"At the shore, I jumped in a big ocean wa..."	*Wave.*
"On my birthday, will you bake me a ca...?"	*Cake.*
"You have a big smile on your fa...!"	*Face.*

Read-Aloud Time Read a Story or Poem

Read aloud to your child for twenty minutes.

Lesson 45: Lowercase S

Lesson 46 - Lowercase T

This lesson will teach lowercase letter t and a new final sounds game.

You will need: *My Book of Letters* pages 111 and 113

Letter of the Day   Sing the Alphabet Song

Sing the Alphabet Song with your child. Point to the letters on the Lowercase Letter Chart as each letter is named.

"Today's letter is t!" Have your child find the letter t on the letter chart.

Complete Letter Activities for Lowercase T

Read the poems for the letter t on pages 83-86 of *Lizard Lou*. Point out the drawings and mention the items that start with the letter t:

"/t/.../t/...*turtle* starts with t."
"/t/.../t/...*tent* starts with t."
"/t/.../t/...*toad* starts with t."

Have your child do the ABC Craft Sheet for lowercase letter t. Ask your child, "What letter does *tent* start with?"

Choose one or more activities from page 195 and complete them with your child.

Letter of the Day
(continued)

Have your child complete the sheet "Circle the t."

The letter t has two basic shapes: *t* and t. The first shape is most commonly used in handwriting and informal fonts. The second shape, t, is used in most text.

Use your judgment as to whether it is a good time to introduce this sheet to your child. You can use this sheet today or save it until your child is ready.

Language Exploration

Play "Snack Time" with Ziggy

"Ziggy would like to tell us what he wants for lunch, but he keeps forgetting to finish his words. Can you guess what Ziggy is trying to say?"

Puppet: "I'd like a cupca..."
Child: *Cupcake!*
Teacher: "What sound did Ziggy leave out?"
Child: */k/.*

"Very good! Let's help him some more."

Continue the activity using the sentences below.

Ziggy says:	Your child says:
"I'd like some jam on toas..."	*Toast.*
"May I have some tomato sou...?"	*Soup.*
"I'd like some corn on the co..."	*Cob.*
"And maybe a little lettuce sala..."	*Salad.*
"To drink, I'd like a tall glass of mil..."	*Milk.*
"And for dessert, a small piece of chocola...!"	*Chocolate.*

Lesson 46: Lowercase T

Read-Aloud Time   Read a Story or Poem

Read aloud to your child for twenty minutes.

 Experiment with using expression when you read aloud. You'll capture your child's attention, and your child will enjoy the extra effort!

There are many things you can do to bring words and stories to life. Here are a few examples:

- If a character utters a word in surprise, make a face to show surprise.
- Try changing your voice to match a character, from an old man to a little mouse.
- If the story is suspenseful, bring a suspenseful tone into your reading.
- Let your child feel the rhythmic words as you follow the heroine in *Madeline* through her experiences as a schoolgirl in Paris.
- When you share the tribulations of Alexander in *Alexander and the Terrible, Horrible, No Good, Very Bad Day* by Judith Viorst, let your child sense Alexander's frustration through your voice.
- When you read the words of the two hippopotamuses in *George and Martha* by James Marshall, give George a slightly deeper voice and Martha a slightly higher voice.

Just a warning, though: getting overdramatic as you read can take away from the storyline. A little dab will do you!

Lesson 46: Lowercase T

Lesson 47 - Lowercase U

This lesson will teach lowercase letter u and a new final sounds game.

You will need: *My Book of Letters* page 115, ten small toys

Letter of the Day   Sing the Alphabet Song

Sing the Alphabet Song with your child. Point to the letters on the Lowercase Letter Chart as each letter is named.

"Today's letter is u!" Have your child find the letter u on the letter chart.

Complete Letter Activities for Lowercase U

Read the poems for the letter u on pages 87-90 of *Lizard Lou*. Point out the drawings and mention the items that start with the letter u:

"What part of a cow does milk come from?" *Udder.*

"This strange guest wouldn't *utter* his name. /ŭ/... /ŭ/...*utter.*"

"Did the writer think that these pants were pretty or ugly?" *Ugly.*

Have your child do the ABC Craft Sheet for lowercase letter u. Ask your child, "What letter does *udder* start with?"

Choose one or more activities from page 195 and complete them with your child.

Language Exploration	Play "Echo" with Ziggy

Before starting this activity, take out ten small toys like wooden blocks or toy cars. These toys will be used to keep score during the game.

"Today we are going to play a game called 'Echo' with Ziggy. I will say a word, and you and Ziggy will take turns repeating the last sound of the word, like an echo. Ziggy will show you how."

Teacher: "Peach. What is the last sound?"
Puppet: "/ch/."
Teacher: "Space."
Puppet: "/s/."

"Very good! Now let's take turns. Each time one of you echos the correct sound, you get a toy. Whoever has the most at the end wins!"

Continue the activity using the words below. Have Ziggy make a mistake now and then so that the child wins the game.

You say:	Your child/Ziggy says:
"Laugh."	/f/.
"Cave."	/v/.
"Plop."	/p/.
"Sack."	/k/.
"Moon."	/n/.
"Zipper."	/r/.
"Slide."	/d/.
"Buzz."	/z/.
"Club."	/b/.
"Frog."	/g/.

Read-Aloud Time Read a Story or Poem

Read aloud to your child for twenty minutes.

Lesson 48 - Lowercase V

This lesson will teach lowercase letter v and a new middle sounds game.

You will need: *My Book of Letters* page 117

Letter of the Day   Sing the Alphabet Song

Sing the Alphabet Song with your child. Point to the letters on the Lowercase Letter Chart as each letter is named.

"Today's letter is v!" Have your child find the letter v on the letter chart.

Complete Letter Activities for Lowercase V

Read the poems for the letter v on pages 91-94 of *Lizard Lou*. Point out the drawings and mention the items that start with the letter v:

"/v/.../v/...*vulture* starts with v."
"/v/.../v/...*vase* starts with v."
"In this picture, the boy is skipping stones across the water. He is pretending that they are *vessels*. A *vessel* is a boat. /v/.../v/...*vessel* starts with v."

Have your child do the ABC Craft Sheet for lowercase letter v. Ask your child, "What letter does *vase* start with?"

Choose one or more activities from page 195 and complete them with your child.

Language Exploration

Play "Listen for the Sound" with Ziggy

"Ziggy likes the sound of /ā/ today. Listen carefully. Whenever he says a word that has the sound of /ā/, clap for him. Let's give it a try."

This is the first activity in which the child is listening for the sound in the *middle* of the word.

Puppet: "Make."
Child claps.
Puppet: "Pie."
Child does not clap.

"Good!"

Continue the activity using the words below.

| lake | maple | clock | rain | shoe | whale |
| teeth | radio | jump | trip | staple | sailboat |

Read-Aloud Time

Read a Story or Poem

Read aloud to your child for twenty minutes.

Encourage your children to pretend to write. They can pretend to write a letter, a caption on a drawing, a grocery list, and so on. At this stage, they probably won't be able to actually write or read what they wrote down, but it is healthy for them to pretend! Pretending is a great sign of "motivation to read," one of the Big Five Skills™.

Lesson 48: Lowercase V

Lesson 49 - Lowercase W

This lesson will teach lowercase letter w.

You will need: *My Book of Letters* page 119

Letter of the Day   Sing the Alphabet Song

Sing the Alphabet Song with your child. Point to the letters on the Lowercase Letter Chart as each letter is named.

"Today's letter is w!" Have your child find the letter w on the letter chart.

Complete Letter Activities for Lowercase W

Read the poems for the letter w on pages 95-98 of *Lizard Lou*. Point out the drawings and mention the items that start with the letter w:
"/w/.../w/...*wave* starts with w."
"/w/.../w/...*worm* starts with w."
"/w/.../w/...*window* starts with w."

Have your child do the ABC Craft Sheet for lowercase letter w. Ask your child, "What letter does *wave* start with?"

Choose one or more activities from page 195 and complete them with your child.

Language Exploration	## Play "Listen for the Sound" with Ziggy

Language Exploration

Play "Listen for the Sound" with Ziggy

"Today Ziggy likes the sound of /ē/. Listen carefully. Whenever he says a word that has the sound of /ē/, jump up. Let's try."

Puppet: "Trees."
Child jumps up.
Puppet: "Mice."
Child does not jump up.

Continue the activity using the words below.

corn	leaf	bees	train	wheat	star
feet	tent	road	speed	meet	hat

Read-Aloud Time

Read a Story or Poem

Read aloud to your child for twenty minutes.

Lesson 50 - Lowercase X

This lesson will teach lowercase letter x.

You will need: *My Book of Letters* page 121

Letter of the Day   Sing the Alphabet Song

Sing the Alphabet Song with your child. Point to the letters on the Lowercase Letter Chart as each letter is named.

"Today's letter is x!" Have your child find the letter x on the letter chart.

Complete Letter Activities for Lowercase X

Read the poems for the letter x on pages 99-102 of *Lizard Lou*. Point out the drawings and mention the items that end with the letter x:

"/ks/.../ks/...*box* ends with x."
"/ks/.../ks/...*ax* ends with x."
"/ks/.../ks/...*lynx* ends with x."

Have your child do the ABC Craft Sheet for lowercase letter x. Ask your child, "What letter does *ax* end with?"

Choose one or more activities from page 195 and complete them with your child.

| Language Exploration | ## Play "Listen for the Sound" with Ziggy |

Language Exploration

Play "Listen for the Sound" with Ziggy

"Today Ziggy likes the sound of /ī/. Listen carefully. Whenever he says a word that has the sound of /ī/, touch your toes. Let's try."

Puppet: "Light."
Child touches his toes.
Puppet: "Rat."
Child does not touch his toes.

Continue the activity using the words below.

pine	chest	stripe	night	grain	hive
big	push	bike	keep	nine	stop

Read-Aloud Time

Read a Story or Poem

Read aloud to your child for twenty minutes.

> If you have a baby in your household, you should start the habit of reading aloud to him or her, too! Choose a colorful, sturdy board book to read aloud. At first, you may only be able to keep your baby's attention for a few minutes, but this time will gradually increase as you enjoy more books together.

Lesson 51 - Lowercase Y

This lesson will teach lowercase letter y.

You will need: *My Book of Letters* pages 123 and 125

Letter of the Day   Sing the Alphabet Song

Sing the Alphabet Song with your child. Point to the letters on the Lowercase Letter Chart as each letter is named.

"Today's letter is y!" Have your child find the letter y on the letter chart.

Complete Letter Activities for Lowercase Y

Read the poems for the letter y on pages 103-106 of *Lizard Lou*. Point out the drawings and mention the items that start with the letter y:
> "/y/.../y/...*yarn* starts with y."
> "/y/.../y/...*yo-yo* starts with y."
> "/y/.../y/...*yawn* starts with y."

Have your child do the ABC Craft Sheet for lowercase letter y. Ask your child, "What letter does *yarn* start with?"

Choose one or more activities from page 195 and complete them with your child.

Letter of the Day
(continued)

Have your child complete the sheet "Circle the y."

The letter y has two basic shapes: 𝑦 and y. The first shape is most commonly used in handwriting and informal fonts. The second shape, y, is used in most text.

Use your judgment as to whether it is a good time to introduce this sheet to your child. You can use this sheet today or save it until your child is ready.

Language Exploration

Play "Listen for the Sound" with Ziggy

"Today Ziggy likes the sound of /ō/. Listen carefully. Whenever he says a word that has the sound of /ō/, say *Ding-dong*! Let's try."

Puppet: "Boat."
Child says Ding-dong.
Puppet: "Rabbit."
Child does not say Ding-dong.

Continue the activity using the words below.

rose	float	kite	wait	coal	hope
last	rock	note	soap	red	pole

Read-Aloud Time — Read a Story or Poem

Read aloud to your child for twenty minutes.

Lesson 52 - Lowercase Z

This lesson will teach lowercase letter z.

You will need: *My Book of Letters* page 127

Letter of the Day   Sing the Alphabet Song

Sing the Alphabet Song with your child. Point to the letters on the Lowercase Letter Chart as each letter is named.

"Today's letter is z!" Have your child find the letter z on the letter chart.

Complete Letter Activities for Lowercase Z

Read the poems for the letter z on pages 107-110 of *Lizard Lou*. Point out the drawings and mention the items that start with the letter z:

"/z/.../z/...*zipper* starts with z."
"/z/.../z/...*zebra* starts with z."
"/z/.../z/...*zero* starts with z."

Have your child do the ABC Craft Sheet for lowercase letter z. Ask your child, "What letter does *zipper* start with?"

Choose one or more activities from page 195 and complete them with your child.

Language Exploration

Play "Silly Mistakes" with Ziggy

Have Ziggy read a familiar poem or story to your child. As the puppet reads, have him make silly mistakes that your child will be able to catch. You can use the following poems, or you can use one of your child's favorite books.

Hear are the corrections for Ziggy's mistakes:

1. Jack and Jill went up the **hill** to fetch a pail of **water**.

2. ...the old **man** is snoring.

3. Mary had a little **lamb**...
   ...its fleece was white as **snow**. Everywhere that **Mary** went...

4. ...have you any **wool**? ...and one for the little **boy**...

Jack and Jill
Jack and Jill went up the **fill**
to fetch a pail of **lemonade**.
Jack fell down and broke his crown,
and Jill came tumbling after.

It's Raining, It's Pouring
It's raining, it's pouring,
the old **van** is snoring.
He bumped his head and went to bed
and couldn't get up in the morning.

Mary Had a Little Lamb
Mary had a little **ham**, little **ham**,
   little **ham**,
Mary had a little **ham**,
its fleece was white as **go**.
Everywhere that **Harry** went,
   Harry went, **Harry** went,
everywhere that **Harry** went,
the lamb was sure to go.

Baa, Baa, Black Sheep
Baa, baa, black sheep,
have you any **pickles**?
Yes sir, yes sir,
three bags full!
One for the master,
one for the dame,
and one for the little **toy**
who lives down the lane.

Read-Aloud Time   Read a Story or Poem

Read aloud to your child for twenty minutes.

Do you tend to fall asleep easily while reading aloud? If so, here are some tips that may help you.

- Try reading at a different time of day, when you have more energy.
- Don't lie down while reading.
- Think about what you are reading.
- Are your eyes fatigued? If so, you may need reading glasses.
- Read with extra drama.
- Take sips of ice water between pages.

Part 3
The Sounds of the Letters

Tips for Part 3 (Lessons 53–78)

- **The main focus of Part 3 is the sounds of the letters.** Your child will learn the most common sound for each letter of the alphabet.

- **Simple hand motions are used to help illustrate the short vowel sounds of <u>a</u>, <u>e</u>, <u>i</u>, <u>o</u>, and <u>u</u>.** The short vowel sounds are more difficult for children to remember. Using this multisensory method, however, makes it easier for children to recall the sounds later.

- **To hear pronunciations of each of the letter sounds, refer to the CD-ROM called _Letter Sounds A to Z_.**

- **You will need the books _The Zigzag Zebra_ and _Lizard Lou_ for this section.**

Lesson 53 - The Sound of /ă/

This lesson will teach the sound of /ă/.

You will need: Letter Sound Card for <u>a</u>, *My Book of Letters* page 129

Sound of the Day

The letter <u>a</u> has three main sounds: /ă/ as in *apple*, /ā/ as in *acorn*, and /ah/ as in *father*. In this lesson, your child will learn the most common sound for <u>a</u>.

Be sure to listen to the correct pronunciation of /ă/ on the CD-ROM called *Letter Sounds A to Z*.

In *All About Spelling* Level 1, your child will learn the three main sounds for the letter <u>a</u>.

Introduce the Sound of /ă/

Take out the Letter Sound Card for <u>a</u> from your Activity Box and hold it up.

"Today's sound is /ă/. What is the first sound in *apple*? /ă/."

Cup your hand as if you are holding an apple. "When we say /ă/, let's pretend that we are holding an apple. Say the sound of <u>a</u> like this: /ă/–/ă/–apple." *Child pretends to hold an apple and says /ă/–/ă/–apple.*

Complete Sound Activities for /ă/

Turn to page 9 of *The Zigzag Zebra*. "Let's name everything we see on this page." Possible answers include *alligator*, *turtle*, *spiderweb*, *sand*, and *grass*.

"What do you see that starts with /ă/?" *Alligator.*

Have your child do the Sound Match-up Sheet for short <u>a</u>. These three drawings start with the sound of /ă/:

alligator

ant

astronaut

Play "What Am I?"

Share the following story with your child.

"Imagine that you are in a spaceship. You are weightless, and you are floating around. You always wanted to go into outer space. You are glad to be an /ă/–/ă/–astronaut."

Now share the following riddles with your child.

"I am thinking of a word that starts with /ă/."

Riddle 1: "I am something to eat. I am usually red. I am round. I grow on trees. Can you guess what I am?" *Apple.*

Riddle 2: "I crawl on the ground. I am very small and have six legs. When some people see me, they want to step on me. I am usually black and shiny. Can you guess what I am?" *Ant.*

Tasty Alphabet Time

If you have the opportunity today, work one of these foods into your meals or snacks:

- Apple slices
- Apricots
- Animal crackers
- Ants on a Log: spread peanut butter on celery sticks and top with raisins

Emphasize the first sound in the name of each food: /ă/.

Read-Aloud Time ## Read a Story or Poem

Read aloud to your child for twenty minutes.

Lesson 54 - The Sound of /b/

This lesson will teach the sound of /b/.

You will need: Letter Sound Card for <u>b</u>, *My Book of Letters* page 131

Sound of the Day

If you wish, you can review the **Tip!** Letter Sound Card for <u>a</u>, too. But keep this activity light and fun. Don't turn it into a drill.

This activity is meant to be an introduction to the letter sounds, so you don't have to work for mastery. Mastery will be achieved in *All About Reading* Level 1.

Introduce the Sound of /b/

Take out the Letter Sound Card for <u>b</u> from your Activity Box and hold it up.

"Today's sound is /b/. What is the first sound in *bat*? /b/.

Complete Sound Activities for /b/

Turn to page 14 of *The Zigzag Zebra*. "Let's name everything we see on this page." Possible answers include *grass*, *bees*, *bears*, *berries*, *bibs*, and *flowers*.

"What do you see that starts with /b/?" *Bees, bears, berries, bibs.*

Have your child do the Sound Match-up Sheet for <u>b</u>. These three drawings start with the sound of /b/:

   boat
   bus
   bee

Language Exploration

Play "What Am I?"

Share the following story with your child.

"Think about when you get into bed at night. Sometimes you feel cold and you like to cover up with something. It is soft and snuggly. You are glad that you have a /b/–/b/–blanket."

Now share the following riddles with your child.

"I am thinking of a word that starts with /b/."

> **Riddle 1:** "I am smaller than you. I need help to eat. I do not walk or talk yet. Sometimes I need a diaper change. Can you guess what I am?" *Baby*.

> **Riddle 2:** "I am something to eat. I am a piece of fruit. I am long and yellow. Monkeys like to eat me, too! Can you guess what I am?" *Banana*.

Tasty Alphabet Time

If you have the opportunity today, work one of these foods into your meals or snacks:

- Bread and butter
- Bananas
- Biscuits
- Beets
- Blueberries

Emphasize the first sound in the name of each food: /b/.

Read-Aloud Time   Read a Story or Poem

Read aloud to your child for twenty minutes.

Lesson 54: The Sound of /b/

Lesson 55 - The Sound of /k/ Spelled with a C

This lesson will teach the sound of /k/.

You will need: Letter Sound Card for <u>c</u>, *My Book of Letters* page 133

Sound of the Day

The letter <u>c</u> has two sounds: /k/ as in *cow* and /s/ as in *cent*. In this lesson, your child will learn the most common sound for <u>c</u>.

In *All About Spelling* Level 1, your child will learn both sounds for the letter <u>c</u>.

Introduce the Sound of /k/

Take out the Letter Sound Card for <u>c</u> from your Activity Box and hold it up.

"Today's sound is /k/. What is the first sound in *cow*? /k/."

Complete Sound Activities for /k/

Turn to page 16 of *The Zigzag Zebra*. "Let's name everything we see on this page." Possible answers include *cats*, *candy*, *crumbs*, *cookies*, *jar*, and *whiskers*.

"What do you see that starts with /k/?" *Cats, cookies, candy, crumbs.*

Have your child do the Sound Match-up Sheet for <u>c</u>. These three drawings start with the sound of /k/:

   clock
   crib
   cup

**Language
Exploration**

Play "What Am I?"

Share the following story with your child.

"Imagine you are sitting at the table eating supper. You have some chicken on your plate and some noodles. There are also vegetables on your plate. They are orange and tasty. On your plate are some /k/–/k/– carrots."

Now share the following riddles with your child.

"I am thinking of a word that starts with /k/."

> **Riddle 1:** "I am often on top of birthday cakes. You sing 'Happy Birthday' when someone lights me. Can you guess what I am?" *Candle.*

> **Riddle 2:** "You know I am there when someone says 'Look at me and smile!' Sometimes I flash. I am used to take your picture. Can you guess what I am?" *Camera.*

Tasty Alphabet Time

If you have the opportunity today, work one of these foods into your meals or snacks:

- Carrots
- Cookies
- Cucumbers
- Cauliflower
- Cabbage
- Corn

Emphasize the first sound in the name of each food: /k/.

Read-Aloud Time ## Read a Story or Poem

Read aloud to your child for twenty minutes.

Lesson 55: The Sound of /k/

Lesson 56 - The Sound of /d/

This lesson will teach the sound of /d/.

You will need: Letter Sound Card for <u>d</u>, *My Book of Letters* page 135

Sound of the Day   Introduce the Sound of /d/

Take out the Letter Sound Card for <u>d</u> from your Activity Box and hold it up.

"Today's sound is /d/. What is the first sound in *deer*? /d/."

Complete Sound Activities for /d/

Turn to page 21 of *The Zigzag Zebra*. "Let's name everything we see on this page." Possible answers include *balls*, *dogs*, *hat*, *dress*, and *stairstep*.

"What do you see that starts with /d/?" *Dogs, dress.*

Have your child do the Sound Match-up Sheet for <u>d</u>. These three drawings start with the sound of /d/:

dog
duck
dinosaur

Language Exploration

Play "What Am I?"

Share the following story with your child.

"Imagine that you are at a museum. There are interesting things everywhere you look. Many children are looking at a huge model of a reptile that used to live long ago. They are looking at a /d/–/d/–dinosaur."

Now share the following riddles with your child.

"I am thinking of a word that starts with /d/."

Riddle 1: "I am covered in feathers. I swim in the water. When I talk, I say 'quack, quack!' Can you guess what I am?" *Duck.*

Riddle 2: "Many people eat me for breakfast. I am round and have a hole in my middle. I often have icing on top. I am very sweet. Can you guess what I am?" *Doughnut.*

Tasty Alphabet Time

If you have the opportunity today, work one of these foods into your meals or snacks:

- Doughnuts
- Dip for vegetables or crackers
- Dill pickles
- Dumplings

Emphasize the first sound in the name of each food: /d/.

Read-Aloud Time

Read a Story or Poem

Read aloud to your child for twenty minutes.

Lesson 56: The Sound of /d/

Lesson 57 - The Sound of /ĕ/

This lesson will teach the sound of /ĕ/.

You will need: Letter Sound Card for e, *My Book of Letters* pages 137 and 139

Sound of the Day

> The letter e has two main sounds: /ĕ/ as in *echo* and /ē/ as in *even*. In this lesson, your child will learn the most common sound for e.
>
> In *All About Spelling* Level 1, your child will learn both of the main sounds for the letter e.

Introduce the Sound of /ĕ/

Take out the Letter Sound Card for e from your Activity Box and hold it up.

"Today's sound is /ĕ/. What is the first sound in *echo*? /ĕ/."

Cup your hand to your ear as if you are listening to an echo. "When we say /ĕ/, let's pretend that we are listening to an echo. Say the sound of e like this: /ĕ/–/ĕ/–echo." *Child pretends to listen for an echo and says* /ĕ/–/ĕ/–echo.

Complete Sound Activities for /ĕ/

Turn to page 24 of *Lizard Lou*. "Let's name everything we see on this page." Possible answers include *boy*, *echo*, *trees*, *hills*, and *mountains*.

"What do you see that starts with /ĕ/?" *Echo*.

Have your child do the Sound Match-up Sheet for short e. These three drawings start with the sound of /ĕ/:

elephant
eggs
elbow

Language Exploration

Find the Letter E

Have your child find and color all of the capital and lowercase e's on the Letter E Activity Sheet, and then guess the animal revealed.

Tasty Alphabet Time

If you have the opportunity today, work one of these foods into your meals or snacks:

- Eggs: deviled, hard-boiled, fried
- Egg salad
- Eggplant

Emphasize the first sound in the name of each food: /ĕ/.

Read-Aloud Time ### Read a Story or Poem

Read aloud to your child for twenty minutes.

Lesson 58 - The Sound of /f/

This lesson will teach the sound of /f/.

You will need: Letter Sound Card for f, *My Book of Letters* page 141

Sound of the Day   Introduce the Sound of /f/

Take out the Letter Sound Card for f from your Activity Box and hold it up.

"Today's sound is /f/. What is the first sound in *fish*? /f/.

Complete Sound Activities for /f/

Turn to page 30 of *The Zigzag Zebra*. "Let's name everything we see on this page." Possible answers include *frog, fish, grass, spiderweb, lily pads, water,* and *birds*.

"What do you see that starts with /f/?" *Frog, fish.*

Have your child do the Sound Match-up Sheet for f. These three drawings start with the sound of /f/:

    fan
    fox
    flag

Language Exploration

Play "What Am I?"

Share the following story with your child.

"Imagine you live in the country. Next to your house is a big barn. You take care of lots of animals like cows and pigs. You grow crops like corn and potatoes. You are a /f/–/f/–farmer."

Now share the following riddles with your child.

"I am thinking of a word that starts with /f/."

> **Riddle 1:** "You use me to pick things up. You hold things with me. You can use me to count up to ten. I am part of your hands. Can you guess what I am?" *Fingers.*

> **Riddle 2:** "I am part of a bird. I am very soft. I come in different sizes and colors. I make a bird look pretty and keep him warm. Without me, a bird could not fly. Can you guess what I am?" *Feathers.*

Tasty Alphabet Time

If you have the opportunity today, work one of these foods into your meals or snacks:

- Fruit
- Figs
- Fish
- French fries
- Fried rice

Emphasize the first sound in the name of each food: /f/.

Read-Aloud Time

Read a Story or Poem

Read aloud to your child for twenty minutes.

Lesson 59 - The Sound of /g/

This lesson will teach the sound of /g/.

You will need: Letter Sound Card for g, *My Book of Letters* page 143

Sound of the Day

The letter g has two sounds: /g/ as in *goose* and /j/ as in *gem*. In this lesson, your child will learn the most common sound for g.

In *All About Spelling* Level 1, your child will learn both sounds for the letter g.

Introduce the Sound of /g/

Take out the Letter Sound Card for g from your Activity Box and hold it up.

"Today's sound is /g/. What is the first sound in *goose*? /g/.

Complete Sound Activities for /g/

Turn to page 14 of *Lizard Lou.* "Let's name everything we see on this page." Possible answers include *grass*, *rabbit*, *goose*, and *birds*.

"What do you see that starts with /g/?" *Goose, grass.*

Have your child do the Sound Match-up Sheet for g. These three drawings start with the sound of /g/:

    goat
    gun
    game

Language Exploration

Play "What Am I?"

Share the following story with your child.

"Imagine you are making a craft. You would like to stick two pieces of paper together. You reach for a bottle and squeeze a small amount of white liquid onto one of the papers. This liquid will get very sticky as it dries. What did you just use? You used /g/–/g/–glue."

Now share the following riddles with your child.

"I am thinking of a word that starts with /g/."

Riddle 1: "You like to put a piece of this in your mouth. It tastes good, but you do not swallow it. Instead, you chew it for a long time. Some people can blow big bubbles with it. Can you guess what I am thinking of?" *Gum.*

Riddle 2: "I am thinking of a color. You see this color in the trees and on the grass. Peas are this color. Can you guess what color I am thinking of?" *Green.*

Tasty Alphabet Time

If you have the opportunity today, work one of these foods into your meals or snacks:

- Grapes
- Graham crackers
- Garlic
- Gumdrops
- Grapefruit

Emphasize the first sound in the name of each food: /g/.

Read-Aloud Time

Read a Story or Poem

Read aloud to your child for twenty minutes.

Lesson 59: The Sound of /g/

Lesson 60 - The Sound of /h/

This lesson will teach the sound of /h/.

You will need: Letter Sound Card for <u>h</u>, *My Book of Letters* page 145

Sound of the Day Introduce the Sound of /h/

Take out the Letter Sound Card for <u>h</u> from your Activity Box and hold it up.

"Today's sound is /h/. What is the first sound in *hat*? /h/.

Complete Sound Activities for /h/

Turn to page 38 of *The Zigzag Zebra*. "Let's name everything we see on this page." Possible answers include *hippo, soap, fish, rubber ducky, waves,* and *bubbles.*

"What do you see that starts with /h/?" *Hippo.*

Have your child do the Sound Match-up Sheet for <u>h</u>. These three drawings start with the sound of /h/:
> *house*
> *ham*
> *hill*

Play "What Am I?"

Share the following story with your child.

"Imagine that you want to build a stool to sit on. You will need some wood. You will need a saw and some nails. You will also need a special tool that has a wood handle and a metal head. You will use this tool to pound in the nails. This tool is a /h/–/h/–hammer."

Now share the following riddles with your child.

"I am thinking of a word that starts with /h/."

Riddle 1: "I am a golden color and taste sweet. I taste good on toast in the morning. I am made by the honeybees that fly from flower to flower. Can you guess what I am?" *Honey.*

Riddle 2: "I am a big animal. I have a mane and a long tail. I have hooves and can gallop very fast. You can put a saddle on me, and I'll give you a ride. Can you guess what I am?" *Horse.*

Tasty Alphabet Time

If you have the opportunity today, work one of these foods into your meals or snacks:

- Honey
- Honeydew melon
- Hamburgers
- Hotdogs
- Ham

Emphasize the first sound in the name of each food: /h/.

Read-Aloud Time   Read a Story or Poem

Read aloud to your child for twenty minutes.

Lesson 61 - The Sound of /ĭ/

This lesson will teach the sound of /ĭ/.

You will need: Letter Sound Card for i, *My Book of Letters* pages 147 and 149

Sound of the Day

The letter i has three main sounds: /ĭ/ as in *itchy*, /ī/ as in *item*, and /ē/ as in *radio*. In this lesson, your child will learn the most common sound for i.

In *All About Spelling* Level 1, your child will learn all three of the main sounds for the letter i.

Introduce the Sound of /ĭ/

Take out the Letter Sound Card for i from your Activity Box and hold it up.

"Today's sound is /ĭ/. What is the first sound in *itchy*? /ĭ/.

Scratch your forearm with your fingertips as if you are itchy. "When we say /ĭ/, let's pretend that we are itchy. Say the sound of i like this: /ĭ/–/ĭ/–itchy." *Child pretends to have an itch and says /ĭ/–/ĭ/–itchy.*

Complete Sound Activities for /ĭ/

Turn to page 41 of *The Zigzag Zebra*. "Let's name everything we see on this page." Possible answers include *inchworms, ski poles, skiis, snowflakes,* and *trees.*

"What do you see that starts with /ĭ/?" *Inchworms.*

Have your child do the Sound Match-up Sheet for short i. These three drawings start with the sound of /ĭ/:

    igloo

    inch

    ink

Language Exploration

Find the Letter I

Have your child find and color all of the capital and lowercase i's on the Letter I Activity Sheet, and then guess the animal revealed.

Tasty Alphabet Time

If you have the opportunity today, work one of these foods into your meals or snacks:

- Incredible pizza: pizza with your child's favorite toppings
- Incredible sandwich: sandwich with your child's favorite fillings

Emphasize the first sound in the name of each food: /ĭ/.

Read-Aloud Time

Read a Story or Poem

Read aloud to your child for twenty minutes.

If you store books in a visible spot, it's more likely that your child will pick one up and start exploring it. Have a special low shelf where your child can keep books. Rotate books off the shelf and onto the coffee table in the family room or the nightstand in your child's bedroom. You may want to keep books in a basket or end table next to the couch so they are handy for read-alouds.

Lesson 61: The Sound of /ĭ/

Lesson 62 - The Sound of /j/

This lesson will teach the sound of /j/.

You will need: Letter Sound Card for j, *My Book of Letters* page 151

Sound of the Day   Introduce the Sound of /j/

Take out the Letter Sound Card for j from your Activity Box and hold it up.

"Today's sound is /j/. What is the first sound in *jam*? /j/.

Complete Sound Activities for /j/

Turn to page 45 of *Lizard Lou*. "Let's name everything we see on this page." Possible answers include *boy, jacket, snowflakes,* and *snowballs.*

"What do you see that starts with /j/?" *Jacket.*

Have your child do the Sound Match-up Sheet for j. These three drawings start with the sound of /j/:

    juice
    jail
    jump

Play "What Am I?"

Share the following story with your child.

"Imagine you are in a place with lots of tall trees and vines. There are monkeys in the trees. Many colorful birds are flying around. You may see a giraffe. You must look out for tigers! It is exciting to be in a /j/–/j/–jungle!"

Now share the following riddles with your child.

"I am thinking of a word that starts with /j/."

> **Riddle 1:** "I am something fun to do outside. I am not a hop. I am not a skip. I am what you do when you want to go over the top of something. I am what you are doing when both feet are off the ground. Can you guess what I am?" *Jump.*

> **Riddle 2:** "I am thinking of something that is fun to eat. It comes in lots of colors like red and orange and yellow and green. This food wiggles when you shake the bowl, and you can see through it. It is good to eat for dessert. Can you guess what I am thinking of?" *Jello.*

Tasty Alphabet Time

If you have the opportunity today, work one of these foods into your meals or snacks:

- Jelly
- Juice
- Jam
- Jello

Emphasize the first sound in the name of each food: /j/.

Read a Story or Poem

Read aloud to your child for twenty minutes.

Lesson 63 - The Sound of /k/ Spelled with a K

This lesson will teach the sound of /k/.

You will need: Letter Sound Card for k, *My Book of Letters* page 153

Sound of the Day

Your child may notice that the letter c also says /k/. In English, there are often several ways to spell the same sound.

Introduce the Sound of /k/

Take out the Letter Sound Card for k from your Activity Box and hold it up.

"Today's sound is /k/. What is the first sound in *kite*? /k/."

Complete Sound Activities for /k/

Turn to page 50 of *The Zigzag Zebra*. "Let's name everything we see on this page." Possible answers include *kangaroo, joey, teddy bear,* and *book.*

"What do you see that starts with /k/?" *Kangaroo.*

Have your child do the Sound Match-up Sheet for k. These three drawings start with the sound of /k/:

king

kangaroo

key

Language Exploration

Play "What Am I?"

Share the following story with your child.

"Imagine you are at a big door. On the other side of the door is something wonderful that you would like to have. But there is a big lock on the door. The door will not open until you have a way to open the lock. What you need is something you hold in your hand. It is called a /k/–/k/–key."

Now share the following riddles with your child.

"I am thinking of a word that starts with /k/."

Riddle 1: "I am a baby animal that is soft and cuddly. I like to run and play. I am very furry and purr when I am happy. Sometimes I will swat you with my paw. Can you guess what I am?" *Kitten.*

Riddle 2: "I am red and I come in a bottle. I taste good. You like to put me on hamburgers and french fries. Can you guess what I am?" *Ketchup.*

Tasty Alphabet Time

If you have the opportunity today, work one of these foods into your meals or snacks:

- Kielbasa
- Kiwi fruit
- Kabobs
- Ketchup

Emphasize the first sound in the name of each food: /k/.

Read-Aloud Time

Read a Story or Poem

Read aloud to your child for twenty minutes.

Lesson 63: The Sound of /k/

Lesson 64 - The Sound of /l/

This lesson will teach the sound of /l/.

You will need: Letter Sound Card for l, *My Book of Letters* page 155

Sound of the Day   Introduce the Sound of /l/

Take out the Letter Sound Card for l from your Activity Box and hold it up.

"Today's sound is /l/. What is the first sound in *leaf*? /l/.

Complete Sound Activities for /l/

Turn to pages 52-54 of *Lizard Lou.* "Let's name everything we see on these three pages." Possible answers include *lion, grass, lizard, rock* and *lollipops.*

"What do you see that starts with /l/?" *Lion, lizard, lollipops.*

Have your child do the Sound Match-up Sheet for l. These three drawings start with the sound of /l/:
>   *lion*
>   *lock*
>   *lick*

Play "What Am I?"

Share the following story with your child.

"Imagine you are in the forest. You have been walking for a long time, and you are getting tired. There are lots of trees and bushes. You would like to rest. Finally you see to something to sit on. You are happy you have found a /l/–/l/–log."

Now share the following riddles with your child.

"I am thinking of a word that starts with /l/."

Riddle 1: "I am part of your body. I am not your head. I am not your arm. I am attached to your feet. You need me to walk and to run and to jump. Can you guess what I am?" *Leg.*

Riddle 2: "I am thinking of something that is tall. It is something you climb when you want to get up high. You must hold on to the sides with your hands to be safe. You climb this one step at a time. Can you guess what I am thinking of?" *Ladder.*

Tasty Alphabet Time

If you have the opportunity today, work one of these foods into your meals or snacks:

- Lemonade
- Licorice
- Lettuce
- Lemons
- Limes
- Lasagna

Emphasize the first sound in the name of each food: /l/.

Read a Story or Poem

Read aloud to your child for twenty minutes.

Lesson 65 - The Sound of /m/

This lesson will teach the sound of /m/.

You will need: Letter Sound Card for <u>m</u>, *My Book of Letters* page 157

Sound of the Day Introduce the Sound of /m/

Take out the Letter Sound Card for <u>m</u> from your Activity Box and hold it up.

"Today's sound is /m/. What is the first sound in *moon*? /m/.

Complete Sound Activities for /m/

Turn to page 58 of *The Zigzag Zebra*. "Let's name everything we see on this page." Possible answers include *cheese, mouse, drink, straw, pillow,* and *quilt.*

"What do you see that starts with /m/?" *Mouse.*

Have your child do the Sound Match-up Sheet for <u>m</u>. These three drawings start with the sound of /m/:

    men
    mop
    mice

Language Exploration

Play "What Am I?"

Share the following story with your child.

"Imagine that you want to have a campfire. You are going to roast marshmallows. You must make a circle of stones to put your fire in. You must also get sticks and logs for the fire. Everyone is waiting to start. But you know that first you must light the fire with a /m/–/m/–match."

Now share the following riddles with your child.

"I am thinking of a word that starts with /m/."

> **Riddle 1:** "You hear me on the radio or stereo. Listening to me can make you want to dance! My sounds might be made with a piano, violin, guitar, drums, or any other instrument. Can you guess what I am?" *Music.*

> **Riddle 2:** "This is something to eat. It is made with noodles and cheese. You eat it with a fork, and it is served hot. Can you guess what I am thinking of?" *Macaroni and cheese.*

Tasty Alphabet Time

If you have the opportunity today, work one of these foods into your meals or snacks:

- Mangoes
- Mushrooms
- Marshmallows
- Milk
- Melba toast
- Mustard
- Macaroni and cheese

Emphasize the first sound in the name of each food: /m/.

Read-Aloud Time

Read a Story or Poem

Read aloud to your child for twenty minutes.

Lesson 66 - The Sound of /n/

This lesson will teach the sound of /n/.

You will need: Letter Sound Card for <u>n</u>, *My Book of Letters* page 159

Sound of the Day   Introduce the Sound of /n/

Take out the Letter Sound Card for <u>n</u> from your Activity Box and hold it up.

"Today's sound is /n/. What is the first sound in *nest*? /n/."

Complete Sound Activities for /n/

Turn to page 60 of *The Zigzag Zebra.* "Let's name everything we see on this page." Possible answers include *nanny goat, tin cans, cat,* and *flowers.*

"What do you see that starts with /n/?" *Nanny goat.* If your child says *goat,* that is correct. Just remind him that some people call female goats by their nickname, *nanny goats.*

Have your child do the Sound Match-up Sheet for <u>n</u>. These three drawings start with the sound of /n/:

   nail
   nut
   net

Language Exploration

Play "What Am I?"

Share the following story with your child.

"Imagine that you are in a hospital. You are helping the doctor take care of people who are sick. You take their temperature and give them pills. This makes them feel better. You are proud to be a /n/–/n/–nurse."

Now share the following riddles with your child.

"I am thinking of a word that starts with /n/."

Riddle 1: "I am skinny and about an inch long. I have a sharp point. I pull thread through cloth when someone sews. I am needed to make all your clothes. Can you guess what I am?" *Needle.*

Riddle 2: "I am part of your face. People need me to hold up their glasses. I am between your eyes. I am what you use to smell. I make you sneeze! Can you guess what I am?" *Nose.*

Tasty Alphabet Time

If you have the opportunity today, work one of these foods into your meals or snacks:

- Nectarines
- Nuts
- Noodles
- Nachos

Emphasize the first sound in the name of each food: /n/.

Read-Aloud Time

Read a Story or Poem

Read aloud to your child for twenty minutes.

Lesson 66: The Sound of /n/

Lesson 67 - The Sound of /ŏ/

This lesson will teach the sound of /ŏ/.

You will need: Letter Sound Card for <u>o</u>, *My Book of Letters* pages 161 and 163

Sound of the Day

The letter <u>o</u> has four main sounds: /ŏ/ as in *otter*, /ō/ as in *open*, /o͞o/ as in *to*, and /ŭ/ as in *oven*. In this lesson, your child will learn the most common sound for <u>o</u>.

In *All About Spelling* Level 1, your child will learn all four of the main sounds for the letter <u>o</u>.

Introduce the Sound of /ŏ/

Take out the Letter Sound Card for <u>o</u> from your Activity Box and hold it up.

"Today's sound is /ŏ/. What is the first sound in *otter*? /ŏ/.

Form an "o" shape with one hand and hold it to your nose. "When we say /ŏ/, let's pretend that we have a nose like an otter. Say the sound of <u>o</u> like this: /ŏ/–/ŏ/–otter." *Child makes an otter nose and says* /ŏ/–/ŏ/–otter.

Complete Sound Activities for /ŏ/

Turn to pages 64-66 of *Lizard Lou*. "Let's name everything we see on these three pages." Possible answers include *otter, water, ocelot, slugs, ox,* and *picture*.

"What do you see that starts with /ŏ/?" *Otter, ocelot, ox.*

Have your child do the Sound Match-up Sheet for short <u>o</u>. These three drawings start with the sound of /ŏ/:

> *ostrich*
> *octopus*
> *olive*

Language Exploration

Find the Letter O

Have your child find and color all of the capital and lowercase <u>o</u>'s on the Letter O Activity Sheet, and then guess the animal revealed.

Tasty Alphabet Time

If you have the opportunity today, work one of these foods into your meals or snacks:

- Olives: green or black
- Omelette

Emphasize the first sound in the name of each food: /ŏ/.

Read-Aloud Time

Read a Story or Poem

Read aloud to your child for twenty minutes.

After the read-aloud today, label some things in your house, such as *couch*, *window*, *lamp*, and *table*. Write each word on a piece of paper or index card, and involve your child in taping it or setting it in place. The purpose is not to have the child read the words or memorize what they look like, but to help him solidify the connection between written text and spoken words.

Your child might also enjoy making a sign for his bedroom. Write the child's name in bold letters—using a capital for the first letter and lowercase for the remaining letters—and let him decorate it as he wishes.

Lesson 68 - The Sound of /p/

This lesson will teach the sound of /p/.

You will need: Letter Sound Card for p, *My Book of Letters* page 165

Sound of the Day   Introduce the Sound of /p/

Take out the Letter Sound Card for p from your Activity Box and hold it up.

"Today's sound is /p/. What is the first sound in *pig*? /p/.

Complete Sound Activities for /p/

Turn to page 70 of *The Zigzag Zebra*. "Let's name everything we see on this page." Possible answers include *porcupines*, *flowers*, and *butterflies*.

"What do you see that starts with /p/?" *Porcupines*.

Have your child do the Sound Match-up Sheet for p. These three drawings start with the sound of /p/:

pins

pen

pumpkin

Language Exploration

Play "What Am I?"

Share the following story with your child.

"Imagine that you are going to visit a friend. You will be sleeping at your friend's house. You will need to pack your toothbrush. You want to bring your own pillow. You might want to bring your favorite toy or your teddy bear. But for sure you want to bring your /p/–/p/–pajamas!"

Now share the following riddles with your child.

"I am thinking of a word that starts with /p/."

Riddle 1: "I am grown in a farmer's field. Some people make pies out of me. I am big and fat and round. I am orange. I am harvested in the fall, and many people carve faces on me and put a candle inside. Can you guess what I am?" *Pumpkin.*

Riddle 2: "I am good to eat for breakfast. I am round and flat. I am often stacked in a pile on the plate. I taste really good with syrup on top. Can you guess what I am?" *Pancake.*

Tasty Alphabet Time

If you have the opportunity today, work one of these foods into your meals or snacks:

- Pineapple
- Pizza
- Popcorn
- Pickles
- Peppers
- Potatoes
- Peaches
- Pears
- Peas

Emphasize the first sound in the name of each food: /p/.

Read-Aloud Time

Read a Story or Poem

Read aloud to your child for twenty minutes.

Lesson 69 - The Sound of /kw/

This lesson will teach the sound of /kw/.

You will need: Letter Sound Card for qu, *My Book of Letters* pages 167 and 169

Sound of the Day

Because this is a more advanced concept, this lesson is optional. You can decide whether you want to teach it to your child or not. If it causes your child any confusion, please skip it.

If you decide not to teach this lesson, please know that this same information will be taught in *All About Reading* Level 1 when your child is more advanced.

Introduce the Sound of /kw/

Take out the Letter Sound Card for qu from your Activity Box and hold it up.

"Today's card has two letters on it: q and u. Q and u work together to make the sound /kw/."

"What is the first sound in *queen?*" */kw/.*

Complete Sound Activities for /kw/

Turn to pages 72-74 of *Lizard Lou.* "Let's name everything we see on these three pages." Possible answers include *ducklings, queen, hearts, tarts,* and *question mark.*

"What do you see that starts with /kw/?" *Queen, question mark.*

"Ducks make a sound that starts with /kw/. What sound is it?" *Quack.*

Have your child do the Sound Match-up Sheet for qu. These three drawings start with the sound of /kw/:
  quack
  quilt
  quail

Find the Letter Q

Have your child find and color all of the capital and lowercase q's on the Letter Q Activity Sheet, and then guess the animal revealed.

Tasty Alphabet Time

If you have the opportunity today, work one of these foods into your meals or snacks:

- Quick bread: types of quick bread include banana bread, pumpkin bread, and nut breads. Quick breads are sweet breads made with baking powder instead of yeast.

Emphasize the first sound in the name of the food: /kw/.

Read-Aloud Time Read a Story or Poem

Read aloud to your child for twenty minutes.

When you are reading aloud, you want your child's full attention. In return, you need to devote your full attention to your child during this twenty-minute period.

One of the biggest distractions in most households is the phone. If your circumstances allow, turn off the phone or promise yourself that you won't answer it during read-alouds.

Here are some more ideas for creating the right environment without distractions:
- Turn off the TV.
- Clear away the toys.
- Make sure older siblings aren't playing video games in the same room.
- Adjust the lighting or curtains so there isn't a glare.

Set yourself up for peaceful reading time, and give your child your undivided attention for twenty minutes.

Lesson 70 - The Sound of /r/

This lesson will teach the sound of /r/.

You will need: Letter Sound Card for r, *My Book of Letters* page 171

Sound of the Day — Introduce the Sound of /r/

Take out the Letter Sound Card for r from your Activity Box and hold it up.

"Today's sound is /r/. What is the first sound in *rake*? /r/.

Complete Sound Activities for /r/

Turn to page 76 of *The Zigzag Zebra*. "Let's name everything we see on this page." Possible answers include *picnic basket, pie, raccoon, blanket, bread, grapes, sandwich,* and *ants.*

"What do you see that starts with /r/?" *Raccoon.*

Have your child do the Sound Match-up Sheet for r. These three drawings start with the sound of /r/:

> *rug*
> *rat*
> *road*

Play "What Am I?"

Share the following story with your child.

"Imagine that it is very hot and you are very thirsty. You want something cold to drink. You walk into the kitchen. You are very happy to know that you can have some juice from the big, cold /r/–/r/– refrigerator!"

Now share the following riddles with your child.

"I am thinking of a word that starts with /r/."

Riddle 1: "I am an animal with brown fur and long ears. I love to hop! I wiggle my nose. And I like to sneak into the garden and eat the lettuce and carrots. Can you guess what I am?" *Rabbit.*

Riddle 2: "I am wet. I fall from the sky and make lots of puddles. I am the reason you have to play inside sometimes. But I also make the garden grow. And after I am gone, sometimes there is a rainbow in the sky. Can you guess what I am?" *Rain.*

Tasty Alphabet Time

If you have the opportunity today, work one of these foods into your meals or snacks:

- Raisins
- Raspberries
- Rice
- Ravioli
- Rolls

Emphasize the first sound in the name of each food: /r/.

Read-Aloud Time Read a Story or Poem

Read aloud to your child for twenty minutes.

Lesson 71 - The Sound of /s/

This lesson will teach the sound of /s/.

You will need: Letter Sound Card for <u>s</u>, *My Book of Letters* page 173

Sound of the Day

The letter <u>s</u> has two sounds: /s/ as in *sun* and /z/ as in *has*. In this lesson, your child will learn the most common sound for <u>s</u>.

In *All About Spelling* Level 1, your child will learn both sounds for the letter <u>s</u>.

Introduce the Sound of /s/

Take out the Letter Sound Card for <u>s</u> from your Activity Box and hold it up.

"Today's sound is /s/. What is the first sound in *sun*? /s/.

Complete Sound Activities for /s/

Turn to page 82 of *Lizard Lou*. "Let's name everything we see on this page." Possible answers include *snowman, snowflakes, scarf, hat, carrot,* and *twigs*.

"What do you see that starts with /s/?" *Snowman, snowflakes, scarf.*

Have your child do the Sound Match-up Sheet for <u>s</u>. These three drawings start with the sound of /s/:
> *sled*
> *sick*
> *six*

Language Exploration

Play "What Am I?"

Share the following story with your child.

"Imagine that you are an animal. You like to eat nuts and acorns. You hide nuts all over outside. You like to run up trees and leap in the branches. You like to chatter at people when they come too close. It is fun being a /s/–/s/–squirrel!"

Now share the following riddles with your child.

"I am thinking of a word that starts with /s/."

> **Riddle 1:** "I am an animal that is long and slinky and skinny. I have scales, not fur. I slither on the ground. I like to hide under rocks. Many people are afraid of me! Can you guess what I am?" *Snake.*

> **Riddle 2:** "I am thinking of something that is slippery when wet. You use it to wash your hands before you eat your meals. Sometimes it makes bubbles. It makes you nice and clean. Can you guess what I am thinking of?" *Soap.*

Tasty Alphabet Time

If you have the opportunity today, work one of these foods into your meals or snacks:

- Sunflower seeds
- Squash
- Strawberries
- Sandwiches
- Spinach
- Spaghetti

Emphasize the first sound in the name of each food: /s/.

Read-Aloud Time

Read a Story or Poem

Read aloud to your child for twenty minutes.

Lesson 71: The Sound of /s/

Lesson 72 - The Sound of /t/

This lesson will teach the sound of /t/.

You will need: Letter Sound Card for t, *My Book of Letters* page 175

Sound of the Day Introduce the Sound of /t/

Take out the Letter Sound Card for t from your Activity Box and hold it up.

"Today's sound is /t/. What is the first sound in *tent*? /t/.

Complete Sound Activities for /t/

Turn to pages 84-86 of *Lizard Lou.* "Let's name everything we see on these three pages." Possible answers include *turtle, boys, backpack, tent, creek, grass, toad,* and *flies.*

"What do you see that starts with /t/?" *Turtle, tent, toad.*

Have your child do the Sound Match-up Sheet for t. These three drawings start with the sound of /t/:
> *tree*
> *tub*
> *truck*

Language Exploration

Play "What Am I?"

Share the following story with your child.

"Imagine you are going on a trip. You are not in a car, but you can look out the window. You are sitting still, but everything is going by very fast. Then you hear a big long whistle. It is fun to travel in a /t/–/t/–train!"

Now share the following riddles with your child.

"I am thinking of a word that starts with /t/."

> **Riddle 1:** "I like to wiggle. You need me to run and walk and jump. It hurts when I am stepped on. There are ten of me, and I am part of your feet. Can you guess what I am?" *Toes.*

> **Riddle 2:** "I start out as a little seed and grow big and tall. I can grow taller than a house. I have lots of leaves. Birds make nests in me, and squirrels climb me. Can you guess what I am?" *Tree.*

Tasty Alphabet Time

If you have the opportunity today, work one of these foods into your meals or snacks:

- Tomato
- Toast
- Tuna fish sandwich
- Tortillas
- Turkey
- Tangerine

Emphasize the first sound in the name of each food: /t/.

Read-Aloud Time

Read a Story or Poem

Read aloud to your child for twenty minutes.

Lesson 73 - The Sound of /ŭ/

This lesson will teach the sound of /ŭ/.

You will need: Letter Sound Card for u, *My Book of Letters* page 177

Sound of the Day

The letter u has three main sounds: /ŭ/ as in *udder*, /ū/ as in *flute*, and /ŏŏ/ as in *put*. In this lesson, your child will learn the most common sound for u.

In *All About Spelling* Level 1, your child will learn all three of the main sounds for the letter u.

Introduce the Sound of /ŭ/

Take out the Letter Sound Card for u from your Activity Box and hold it up.

"Today's sound is /ŭ/. What is the first sound in *udder*? /ŭ/.

Using both hands, do a hand motion like you are milking a cow. "When we say /ŭ/, let's pretend that we are farmers milking a cow. Say the sound of u like this: /ŭ/–/ŭ/–udder." *Child pretends to milk a cow and says /ŭ/–/ŭ/–udder.*

Complete Sound Activities for /ŭ/

Turn to page 90 of *The Zigzag Zebra*. "Let's name everything we see on this page." Possible answers include *penguin, umbrella, scarf, snow, hill,* and *ocean.*

"What do you see that starts with /ŭ/?" *Umbrella.*

Have your child do the Sound Match-up Sheet for u. These three drawings start with the sound of /ŭ/:
  umbrella
  underwear
  up

Language Exploration

Play "What Am I?"

Share the following story with your child.

"Imagine that you are a monkey. You like to swing from tree to tree, and so do all of your monkey friends. You especially like to hang from your tail. When you do, everything looks like it's /ŭ/–/ŭ/–upside down!"

Now share the following riddles with your child.

"I am thinking of a word that starts with /ŭ/."

Riddle 1: "I am thinking of something you wear. You wear them under your other clothes. You wear them every day. No one else is supposed to see them. Can you guess what I am thinking of?" *Underwear.*

Riddle 2: "I am good to have around when it rains. You hold me by the handle. I keep you dry in a rainstorm, but I drip on the floor when you bring me inside. When you don't need me, you can fold me back up. Can you guess what I am?" *Umbrella.*

Tasty Alphabet Time

If you have the opportunity today, work one of these foods into your meals or snacks:

- Upside-down cake
- Upside-down hamburger (or any other food that can be served upside down)

Emphasize the first sound in the name of each food: /ŭ/.

Read-Aloud Time ## Read a Story or Poem

Read aloud to your child for twenty minutes.

Lesson 73: The Sound of /ŭ/

Lesson 74 - The Sound of /v/

This lesson will teach the sound of /v/.

You will need: Letter Sound Card for v, *My Book of Letters* page 179

Sound of the Day   Introduce the Sound of /v/

Take out the Letter Sound Card for v from your Activity Box and hold it up.

"Today's sound is /v/. What is the first sound in *vase*? /v/.

Complete Sound Activities for /v/

Turn to pages 92-96 of *Lizard Lou*. "Let's name everything we see on these three pages." Possible answers include *vulture, vase, picture frame, boat, boy,* and *creek.*

"What do you see that starts with /v/?" *Vulture, vase.*

Have your child do the Sound Match-up Sheet for v. These three drawings start with the sound of /v/:

 volcano

 van

 vacuum

Language Exploration

Play "What Am I?"

Share the following story with your child.

"Imagine that you love taking care of dogs and cats. You help pets stay healthy, and you sometimes have to give them shots. Families bring their sick pets to you, and you make them better. You are glad to be a /v/–/v/–vet."

Now share the following riddles with your child.

"I am thinking of a word that starts with /v/."

Riddle 1: "I clean the carpets or rugs in your house. You plug me in and turn me on, and I make a loud noise as I clean. You push me around and I suck up the dirt. Can you guess what I am?" *Vacuum.*

Riddle 2: "I am a special type of mountain. I am usually tall with a hole in the top. Sometimes hot red lava pours out of me. I make a lot of smoke, and I might even shoot out fire. Can you guess what I am?" *Volcano.*

Tasty Alphabet Time

If you have the opportunity today, work one of these foods into your meals or snacks:

- Vanilla wafers
- Vegetables
- Vanilla pudding

Emphasize the first sound in the name of each food: /v/.

Read-Aloud Time

Read a Story or Poem

Read aloud to your child for twenty minutes.

Lesson 75 - The Sound of /w/

This lesson will teach the sound of /w/.

You will need: Letter Sound Card for <u>w</u>, *My Book of Letters* page 181

Sound of the Day Introduce the Sound of /w/

Take out the Letter Sound Card for <u>w</u> from your Activity Box and hold it up.

"Today's sound is /w/. What is the first sound in *wave*? /w/.

Complete Sound Activities for /w/

Turn to page 98 of *The Zigzag Zebra*. "Let's name everything we see on this page." Possible answers include *walrus, birds,* and *ice.*

"What do you see that starts with /w/?" *Walrus.*

Have your child do the Sound Match-up Sheet for <u>w</u>. These three drawings start with the sound of /w/:
>   *window*
>   *worm*
>   *watch*

Language Exploration

Play "What Am I?"

Share the following story with your child.

"Imagine you have been walking through a desert for days. You are hot, and you are thirsty. The sun has been beating down all day. You are afraid that you might even be lost! Oh, wait, what is that? You see a restaurant in the distance! You can't wait to have a drink of /w/–/w/– water!"

Now share the following riddles with your child.

"I am thinking of a word that starts with /w/."

Riddle 1: "I am something that people wear on their wrists. People look at me so they know what time it is. If they know the time, they won't be late for supper! Can you guess what I am?" *Watch.*

Riddle 2: "You have several of me in your house. I am made of glass, and you can see through me. I keep out the cold and the rain. When I am open, fresh air can come in. Can you guess what I am?" *Window.*

Tasty Alphabet Time

If you have the opportunity today, work one of these foods into your meals or snacks:

- Wheat bread
- Walnuts
- Water
- Watermelon

Emphasize the first sound in the name of each food: /w/.

Read-Aloud Time

Read a Story or Poem

Read aloud to your child for twenty minutes.

Lesson 75: The Sound of /w/

Lesson 76 - The Sound of /ks/

This lesson will teach the sound of /ks/.

You will need: Letter Sound Card for x, *My Book of Letters* pages 183 and 185

Sound of the Day

Introduce the Sound of /ks/

Take out the Letter Sound Card for x from your Activity Box and hold it up.

"Today's sound is /ks/. What is the last sound in *ax*? /ks/.

Complete Sound Activities for /ks/

Turn to page 101 of *The Zigzag Zebra*. "Let's name everything we see on these three pages." Possible answers include *fox, bees, log,* and *hill.*

"What do you see that ends with /ks/?" *Fox.*

Have your child do the Sound Match-up Sheet for x. These three drawings end with the sound of /ks/:

    box
    fox
    ox

Language Exploration

Find the Letter X

Have your child find and color all of the capital and lowercase x's on the Letter X Activity Sheet, and then guess the animal revealed.

Tasty Alphabet Time

If you have the opportunity today, work one of these foods into your meals or snacks:

- Six of anything: six grapes, six crackers, six orange slices

Emphasize the last sound in the name of the food: /ks/.

Read-Aloud Time

Read a Story or Poem

Read aloud to your child for twenty minutes.

 If you normally read in the same place each day, try out a new location today. Try the front porch, a bench at the park, a gazebo, or sitting on the stairs.

Lesson 77 - The Sound of /y/

This lesson will teach the sound of /y/.

You will need: Letter Sound Card for y, *My Book of Letters* page 187

Sound of the Day

The letter y has four sounds: /y/ as in *yarn*, /ĭ/ as in *gym*, /ī/ as in *my*, and /ē/ as in *happy*. In this lesson, your child will learn the most common sound for y.

In *All About Spelling* Level 1, your child will learn all four sounds for the letter y.

Introduce the Sound of /y/

Take out the Letter Sound Card for y from your Activity Box and hold it up.

"Today's sound is /y/. What is the first sound in *yarn*? /y/."

Complete Sound Activities for /y/

Turn to page 105 of *The Zigzag Zebra*. "Let's name everything we see on this page." Possible answers include *yak, yarn, basket,* and *fence.*

"What do you see that starts with /y/?" *Yak, yarn.*

Have your child do the Sound Match-up Sheet for y. These three drawings start with the sound of /y/:

yo-yo

yolk

yawn

Language Exploration

Play "What Am I?"

Share the following story with your child.

"Imagine a place where it is fun to be. You can run and jump. There are birds and butterflies. You can build a snowman in the winter. You can run through the sprinkler in the summer. Your friends can play with you there. Some people have one of these right outside their house. It is a /y/–/y/–yard."

Now share the following riddles with your child.

"I am thinking of a word that starts with /y/."

> **Riddle 1:** "I am a color. I am bright and happy-looking. I am the same color as the sun and a banana. Can you guess what I am?" *Yellow.*

> **Riddle 2:** "I am thinking of a loud noise that you make when you are outside and having fun. It isn't a good idea to do this when you are in the house. Can you guess what kind of sound I am thinking of?" *Yell.*

Tasty Alphabet Time

If you have the opportunity today, work one of these foods into your meals or snacks:

- Yogurt
- Yams

Emphasize the first sound in the name of each food: /y/.

Read-Aloud Time   ## Read a Story or Poem

Read aloud to your child for twenty minutes.

Lesson 78 - The Sound of /z/

This lesson will teach the sound of /z/.

You will need: Letter Sound Card for z, *My Book of Letters* pages 189 and 191

Sound of the Day   Introduce the Sound of /z/

Take out the Letter Sound Card for z from your Activity Box and hold it up.

"Today's sound is /z/. What is the first sound in *zipper*? /z/."

Complete Sound Activities for /z/

Turn to page 108-110 of *Lizard Lou*. "Let's name everything we see on these three pages." Possible answers include *zipper, slippers, zebra, boy, zero, numbers, teddy bear,* and *pillow.*

"What do you see that ends with /z/?" *Zipper, zebra, zero.*

Have your child do the Sound Match-up Sheet for z. These three drawings end with the sound of /z/:

    zero

    zebra

    zoo

Language Exploration

Find the Letter Z

Have your child find and color all of the capital and lowercase z's on the Letter Z Activity Sheet, and then guess the animal revealed.

Tasty Alphabet Time

If you have the opportunity today, work one of these foods into your meals or snacks:

- Zucchini
- Zwieback toast
- Ziti noodles

Emphasize the first sound in the name of each food: /z/.

Read-Aloud Time

Read a Story or Poem

Read aloud to your child for twenty minutes.

Celebrate!

Present Your Student with the Certificate of Achievement

Lesson 78: The Sound of /z/

Part 4
Appendices

Appendix A
More Fun with the Alphabet

These hands-on activities provide multiple ways to interact with the letters of the alphabet. When you use a variety of activities, your children grow in letter knowledge, one of the Big Five Skills™.

 Using your favorite handwriting program, have your child practice letter formation for the Letter of the Day.

 Form the Letter of the Day with pipe cleaners, Wikki Stix®, or toothpicks.

 Stick magnetic letters on the refrigerator and find the Letter of the Day.

 Shape clay, modeling wax, or playdough into letter shapes.

 Go on a Letter Hunt. Look through old magazines to locate examples of the Letter of the Day. Cut out the letters and store them in an envelope for future crafts or paste them to a piece of paper.

 Alphabet Stamps are fun to use. Decorate a greeting card or stationery by stamping it with the Letter of the Day.

 With your pointer finger, trace the Letter of the Day in fingerpaint, pudding, shaving cream, salt, or sand.

Appendix B
The Alphabet Song

Why the Alphabet Song Is Important

The Alphabet Song helps children internalize that each letter has a name. Children who know the names of the letters have three major advantages:

1. They will learn the sounds of the letters much more easily. In contrast, children who don't know the letter names often have tremendous difficulty in learning the sounds of the letters.[1]
2. Children who can easily name the letters of the alphabet have an easier time learning to read.[2]
3. As they learn the letter names, children tend to be more motivated to discover more about the letters and words around them.[3]

Tips for Teaching the Alphabet Song

The Alphabet Song is traditionally sung to the tune of "Twinkle, Twinkle, Little Star." When you sing the song, take care not to run the letters together. Slow down especially when you get to l, m, n, and o. Those four letters run together because they are crammed into only two beats in the song.

If your children don't already know the Alphabet Song, sing it to them (and, eventually, with them) every day. You can sing it during lesson time, before story hour, or even while they wash their hands before meals.

If your child already knows the Alphabet Song, concentrate on separating the letters l, m, n, and o. Also make sure that your child is confident with the end of the Alphabet Song—some children get tangled up with w, x, y, z.

Alternate Tune for the Alphabet Song

To avoid the difficulties of the traditional Alphabet Song, you can sing the alphabet to the tune of "Mary Had a Little Lamb." When sung to this tune, the letters l, m, n, and o are spoken separately. Note that two beats are given to the letter w.

Here's how the alternate tune goes:

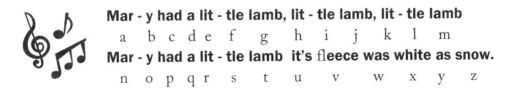

Mar - y had a lit - tle lamb, lit - tle lamb, lit - tle lamb
a b c d e f g h i j k l m
Mar - y had a lit - tle lamb it's fleece was white as snow.
n o p q r s t u v w x y z

---

1 Mason (1980)
2 Bond and Dykstra (1967); Chall (1967)
3 Chomsky (1979); Mason (1980); Read (1971)

Appendix C
References

Adams, Marilyn Jager (1990). *Beginning to read: Thinking and learning about print.* Boston: MIT Press.

Birsh, Judith R. (2005). *Multisensory Teaching of Basic Language Skills,* 2nd ed. Baltimore: Paul H. Brookes Publishing Co.

Blevins, Wiley. (1998). *Phonics from A to Z.* New York: Scholastic.

Bond , Guy L., and Dykstra, Robert (1967). The cooperative research program in first-grade reading instruction. *Reading Research Quarterly, 2,* 5-142.

Chall, Jeanne S. (1967). *Learning to read: The great debate.* New York: McGraw-Hill.

Chomsky, Carol (1979). Approaching reading through invented spelling. In L. B. Resnick and P. A. Weaver (eds.), *Theory and practice of early reading,* vol. 2, 43-65. Hillsdale, NJ: Erlbaum Associates.

Ehri, L.C. (2004). Teaching phonemic awareness and phonics: an explanation of the National Reading Panel meta-analyses. In P. McCardle & V. Chhabra (Eds.), *The voice of evidence in reading research* (pp. 153-186). Baltimore: Paul H. Brookes Publishing Co.

Ehri, L.C., Nunes, S.R., Stahl, S.A., & Willos, D.M. (2001). Systematic phonics instruction helps students learn to read: evidence from the National Reading Panel's meta-analysis. *Review of Educational Research.*

Hall, Susan L. and Moats, Louisa C. (2006). *Straight talk about reading: How parents can make a difference during the early years.* New York: McGraw-Hill.

Mason, Jana M. (1980). When do children begin to read: an exploration of our year-old children's letter and word reading competencies. *Reading Research Quarterly, 15,* 203-227.

National Institute of Child Health and Human Development (NICHD) (2000). *Report of the National Reading Panel: Teaching children to read: An evidence-based assessment of the scientific research literature on reading and its implications for reading instruction: Report of the subgroups* (NIH Publication No. 00-4754). Washington, DC: Government Printing Office.

Read, Charles (1971). Preschool children's knowledge of English phonology. *Harvard Educational Review, 41,* 1-34.

Shaywitz, Sally (2003). *Overcoming dyslexia: A new and complete science-based program for reading problems at any level.* New York: Alfred A. Knopf.

Snow, C.E, Burns, M.S., & Griffin, P. (Eds.). (1998). *Preventing reading difficulties in young children.* Washington, D.C.: National Academies Press.

Stanovich, K.E. (1986). Matthew effects in reading: Some consequences of individual differences in the acquisition of literacy. *Reading Research Quarterly, 21,* 260-406.

Yopp, H. K. (1992). Developing phonemic awareness in young children. *Reading Teacher, 45 (9),* 696-703.

Index

- NOTES -

– NOTES –

- NOTES -

– NOTES –

– NOTES –

– NOTES –